Perfect Tir

How to Make the Right Decisions at the Right Time

by

Margaret Neylon

Strategic Book Group

Strategic Book Group

P.O. Box 333

Durham CT 06422
www.StrategicBookClub.com

ISBN: 978-1-60976-848-5

Dedication

To Dorothy, Elizabeth, Christine, Stefan and Mary, with love.

Contents:

Time is free, but it's priceless.
You can't own it but you can use it.
You can't keep it but you can spend it.
Once you've lost it you can never get it back.

Harvey MacKay

Introduction

Have you ever had a brilliant idea or an innovative plan of action which you have tried to get support to bring into reality, only to be ignored? Then, five or ten years later, someone else brings out a similar idea and makes a great success of it. There's nothing more frustrating!

Have you started a project with great gusto only to let it inexplicably fade into nothing as the weeks go by?

Why does this happen? Why do some people have good, lasting relationships effortlessly, while yours may start with great promise, then die away like a damp squib? Why do others have endless success in their careers while yours amounts to nothing? Is there something lacking in you, or are these things completely out of your control? Have you tried to make major changes in your life on January 1st and found nothing worked? It doesn't mean you're a failure, it simply means you've most likely been doing things at the wrong time!

Generally speaking, we cannot control events which happen, but we always control how we respond to them.

I often say to my clients 'Just because it rains it doesn't mean you have to get wet'. Each of us can make a choice about the rain; do we stay indoors, do we use an umbrella, or do we go outside, unprepared, and get soaking wet? The rain is out of our control, but what we do about it is in our hands. Whether we act quickly, review the situation or completely dismiss it, is up to us. One of the most important aspects of making a success of your plans is timing.

Have you come across this message from Solomon in the Bible? (You'll find the full quotation in the Book of Ecclesiastes 3. 1-8, and the American pop group The Byrds used similar lyrics in their song 'Turn, Turn, Turn'.). Though it was written many years ago, it still holds a vital message for us all:

To everything there is a Season

To every thing there is a season, and a time to every purpose under the heaven:
A time to be born, and a time to die;

a time to plant, and a time to pluck up that which is planted;
A time to kill, and a time to heal;
a time to break down, and a time to build up;
A time to weep, and a time to laugh;
a time to mourn, and a time to dance;
A time to cast away stones, and a time to gather stones together;
a time to embrace, and a time to refrain from embracing;
A time to get, and a time to lose;
a time to keep, and a time to cast away;

Yes, there is a time and a season for everything. Often we feel a failure because we do something and it doesn't work out. However, the reason it doesn't work out may be because it was not the right time to do it. 'Perfect Timing' should give you many opportunities to discover the perfect timing for you to bring a feeling of fulfilment into your life. It's much easier than you may think, once you have an understanding of the basic rules behind numerology, astrology or Celtic beliefs.

The science of Horology – that is breaking down the day and night into seconds, minutes and hours, was invented by mankind during the 13th Century by the Song Dynasty in China. It wasn't brought into general use until the mechanisation of industry in the mid-1800s. In fact, it was the advent of the train network in Britain that first encouraged

London Time which then developed into the clock we know today. Mankind is the only species on Planet Earth which follows seconds, minutes and hours. Until horology was invented by man, everyone followed the seasons and lunar cycles. For instance, did you know that the word 'month' comes from the Latin 'menses' which is another word for 'the Moon'. Just as the tidal waters are affected by the Moon cycle, humans are affected by the highs and lows of the lunar energies too.

Are you aware that you need work only three months of the year? Yes, despite being employed for twelve months of the year, it is necessary only to work one quarter of that time in order to achieve the same results as working for the full year. Why? Because there is a perfect time for certain tasks, and no matter how hard you work at inappropriate times, you do not achieve anything more. That may sound incredible, but you will find it is true when you have read this book and put its suggestions into action for yourself.

Chapter 1

An Introduction to Celtic Timing

In Celtic times, which takes us back many thousands of years, there were specific timings during the year when the people knew what to do and what to expect, and probably just as importantly, what not to do and what not to expect! If you can take yourself back to 5,000 years ago, there was very little outside communication between tribes and certainly little travel except by water, and therefore very little influence between the different groups of settlements. The main outside influence for these pastoral people, who were totally dependent on the weather and the land, were the seasons. The seasons could bring sunshine, brightness, wind, rain, frost, snow and darkness. In order to survive and make the most of what Mother Nature offered them, they divided the year into 'lunations', which followed the progress of the moon throughout the months ('lunar' means 'moon'). As there are thirteen Moons, there were thirteen 'lunations' through the pastoral year. What Lunation were you born under? How has it affected your attitude to life and the lessons you are here to learn? Also, see where you are now in the calendar of Lunations below. If you are currently in 'The Darkest Depths;' (November/December), is it any wonder if you feel a little downhearted? While if you are currently in the time of 'Shoots Show' (April/May), you are probably longing to get out and about a do a spot of gardening! Does this give you any understanding of what to expect and what actions to take or cease? I have included some well-known celebrities further on in this chapter to show some examples of the types of personalities born within these periods.

The Lunations

Timing is all important for the success of your journey. Perhaps you are waiting for the auspicious time before you act, or are impatient to know when something will begin to end. Often you can take the incorrect path simply because you move too quickly, or wait until it's too late for right action! The Lunation symbolises the 'lunar' or emotional/intuitive time either that you were born in or that you are in at present. As mentioned earlier, in the Celtic Year there were thirteen moons in every year, with the New Year commencing at sunset on 31 October. All Celtic Festivals begin at sunset and last until dusk of the following day. Note the names of the months as we know them are as set down by a calendar unknown at this time and, they are set out to start with the New Moon during the month stated, so the Lunation of Seedfall begins with the New Moon at the end of October. The thirteen phases of Lunation are:

1st Moon: Season: Seedfall:
Time: October/November

It's the New Year! The Festival of Samhain (pro. Sow -wen) means 'burning of the bones'. Bone fires (bonfires) light up the darkness, burning the old and allowing space for the new! It is time to turn to the spirit for guidance through the long winter months which lie ahead. Gain knowledge and insight by allowing yourself to receive guidance through meditation and dreams.

If you were born during this time, you may find it difficult to cope with the dark days and nights, and if you ever feel depressed it may be because of the outside influence of the weather. The best approach is to focus on the growth of your spirituality. Pamper yourself during those dark nights, spend time sharing your philosophies and hopes with close friends. Springtime will eventually return!

2nd Moon: Season: Mid-Seedfall:
Time: November

2

Although the days are short and the nights are long, Nature is already preparing for the new year by dropping her seeds for renewed growth. Allow Nature take her course; there is no physical work for you to do, instead tune into your spirit at this time. Ask yourself what should you plant for the new year? Be patient and realise inaction and introspection can be just as important as taking action on occasion!

Those born during Mid-Seedfall need to think ahead. Life is about change and trying to cling on to the past simply won't work. Mid-Seedfall people often have a total change in their lives in their 30s or 40s.

3rd Moon: Season: Darkest Depths:
Time: November/December

Consider living in those years before electricity was invented, long before global communication, when people lived in small communities, unaware of what was happening in the greater world outside. At the time: of the Winter Solstice on the 21st December when the Sun stays static in the sky, they would have been wondering would it ever return with renewed vigour? Trust in support outside of mere mankind is called for at this time!

People celebrating their birthday during the Darkest Depths may yearn for the sun and never quite accept the fact that they are living through such an inhospitable time. It's important to surround yourself with colour. Wear a bright scarf, decorate your home with cheap and cheerful cushions and throws, bring the sun into your life in this way.

4th Moon: Season: Cold Time:
Time: December/January

The Sun is rarely seen and, if it appears, it is weak and stays for only a short time. There is no heat, little light, and it's cold, both inside and outside. Now is the time for asking yourself 'Am I on the right path? Will the light of a new Dawn ever come again? This can be the most difficult time on your journey.

Don't moan if no-one is contacting you. Pick up the phone yourself and make a call! Socialising doesn't have to cost a fortune but it can draw you out of those cold, dark moments you are spending alone. Be pro-active if you want to feel that life-force coursing through your veins!

5th Moon: Season: Stay-Home Time:
Time: January/February

Just when it seems impossible that new life will come into the world, the ewes and cows begin to bring forth new life in the form of lambs and calves, and new milk. The Festival of Oimelc or Imbolc (pro: Immulk), on the eve of 31st January till the eve of 1st February, celebrates the power of Nature and the female creative cycle.

This is a time for nurturing. Most people find it easy to nurture others, but tend to subdue their own needs. It's important that those born within this time of year ensure they take good care of themselves. Natural energy will be at a low ebb so try not to put yourself under unnecessary stress. Remember, in a short while new life will burst forth again!

6th Moon: Season: Time of Ice:
Time: February/March

The days are becoming longer; though there may be ice underfoot it usually melts by noon-time, bringing the promise of renewed warmth. Small shoots and tiny flowers are pushing up from the Earth. Hope begins to grow in your heart. The darkest hours are in the past now. A new surge of life moves through your veins!

Those born during the Time of Ice may need extra support from those around them. Their mentality may veer from total confidence one day to feelings of abject failure the next! Learn to focus on your plans and try not to be distracted by what happened in the past. Yes, it happened, but it belongs to the past, not the present.

7th Moon. Season: Time of Winds:
Time: March/April

4

The Spring Equinox has arrived. You know that the worst is over. You know that the Sun is becoming stronger, that life is renewing itself. You have planted your new crop. Yet still there is uncertainty. Which way to go? There are so many choices! Be advised to stay on the right path, no matter how the wind seems to change its direction!

If you were born at the time when the day and night become equal, it's important to maintain balance in all that you do. You are probably ambitious and quite single-minded, but make sure you don't run rough-shod over those around you! Rather than act like a gale-force wind which blows itself out as rapidly as it began, instead be like a gentle, summer breeze and keep focused on exactly where you wish to go.

8th Moon. Season: Shoots-Show.
Time: April/May

Proof of Nature's goodness is here at last! The shoots of the Spring have pushed through the cold Earth and are now beginning to show their true colours! Your hard labour is beginning to prove worthwhile. The animals are finding new food to feast on, and for you, too, it's a time of celebration! The Festival of Beltaine, (pro: Be-alta-na), offers time for courtship and romance.

Those celebrating their birthday during Shoots-Show usually enjoy a mixture of ambition together with vital energy and enthusiasm. They have great abilities to be successful but may need to be aware of what is happening around them or they could unwittingly damage close relationships.

9th Moon. Season: Time of Brightness.
Time: May/June

Enjoy your just desserts at this time! Tend what you planted in your life. Dispense with weeds which take energy away. Make the most of the long days and the short nights. Be aware that all your hard work will repay you in abundance. Celebrate the Festival of Midsummer on 21 June, the longest day.

The Time of Brightness can be one of the most sociable times of the year, and those born within this Lunation are usually great communicators and often 'the life and soul of the party'. One area they need to focus on, however, is the ability to express how they genuinely feel. It's vital they show their authentic self or they may find it difficult to sustain a long-term relationship.

10th Moon. Season: Horse Time.
Time: June/July

Your crop is ripening in the field. Your stock is looking after its young. All is well in the world. Take time out now, as Nature looks after your needs, to enter into conviviality with others. As in the old days, compete in friendship with others. Your energy, seen here as 'horse-power', is at its peak. Make the most of this time of relaxation.

People born during Horse Time are usually competitive and ambitious. They are sociable characters who like nothing better than to arrange or attend a get-together, but don't expect them to keep all their promises as sometimes they can be a bit frisky and forgo their responsibilities.

11th Moon. Season: Claim Time.
Time: July/August

The eve of 31st July is the Festival of Lughnasagh (pro: Loon asa), celebrating the Sun God Lugh, and it is a time for the celebration of male and female coming together. Claim your right to courtship with another. It is a time for celebrating your own personal energy and also to make agreements for the future.

Claim Time people usually like to settle down in their early years and be part of a loving partnership. They may lack some personal drive or ambition but they will do anything for their loved ones. While they may not fight for themselves, beware causing problems for their partner or children, for they will certainly make their displeasure known!

12th Moon. Season: Arbitration Time.
Time: August/September

Now the harvest is assured. It is not yet right for the picking, but you know for certain it is only a short time before you will benefit from it. Take time out for yourself now, for rest and relaxation. Do research if necessary, and plan for the future, ensuring that all legal matters are worked out in advance.

Knowing precisely where they are and what is expected of them is essential to those born under this Lunation. They don't like to leave things to chance as it makes them feel insecure, and they tend to enjoy learning new things.. The best way to ensure their happiness is to have a strong base, plan ahead and take responsibility for their actions.

13th Moon. Season: Song Time.
Time: September/October

Sing with joy for the harvest that is gifted to you! A feeling of justifiable pride in your work to date is called for at this time. The Autumn Equinox on the 21 September signifies that again the full year is coming to a close and your harvest should be gratefully accepted. The struggle is over! Raise your voice in thanks for the goodness you have been given!

Song Time people are good communicators and often take on other people's issues. They might be the spokesperson for a group or the leader of a debating society or political party. They are usually popular with others and fit in quite easily with other people's expectations.

Some Celebrity Examples

Oprah Winfrey, born on 29th January, came into this world during Stay at Home Time. This could be seen as 'the darkest hour before the dawn' because in the Northern Hemisphere we are usually still in the grip of winter at this time, and there is very little growth to be seen.

7

However, with focus and determination, it is possible to ensure a fine harvest in the future when the soil begins to warm up with the Festival of Oimelc and the springtime sun. Oprah has certainly turned her back on the temptation of seeing herself as a victim of her early experiences and, instead, focused on a positive long-term goal and changed her life in a remarkable way. She has publically stated that she knew she had a choice: to fall into the trap of victimhood or to take responsibility for her life. It's not easy battling against the elements either literally or metaphorically, but Oprah Winfrey is a shining example of someone who did just that. Another woman who was born during Stay at Home Time is Ellen de Generes (26th January). She had quite a struggle in her early years, working in all sorts of jobs such as in a mall, being a house painter and a bar tender. This unpromising start didn't hinder her, though. Instead, she used her early experiences to develop her career in comedy and, with hard work and commitment, has become a major tv star.

As the hours of sunlight begin to slowly increase from mid-February and we move closer to the Vernal Equinox, the 6th Moon brings us into the Time of Ice. Life can still prove to be a struggle yet there is some promise of new growth underfoot. The singer Rihanna (whose birth date is 20th February), has had to make her own sacrifices to see her dreams become a reality. She left her home in Barbados at the age of sixteen to work towards her now dazzling singing career. At that young age she took guidance from record producer, Evan Rogers, and worked long and hard to get the record deal she longed for. The Time of Ice may seem forbidding at first sight but, with support from others, much can be achieved.

Actor George Clooney celebrates his birthday on 6th May, which falls into the Shoots Show lunation. This is, quite literally, the time of year when the growth begins to show and is the time of Bealtine, when our ancestors would have taken time out to socialise after the hard work of sowing the fields and tending the newly-born animals. It's a time for relaxation and socialising, and people born around this time are usually easy going, convivial and ambitious. Sometimes, however, that ambition can cause problems in intimate relationships where one person might be present while the other is more tuned in to climbing their personal ladder to success. UK former Prime Minister Tony Blair shares his birthday with George Clooney on 6th May.

The Sun certainly seems to shine on those born within the Claim Time lunation, the time to celebrate Lughnasagh, named after the Celtic Sun God Lugh. Both US President Barack Obama (4th August) and President Bill Clinton (19th August) were blessed to be born under this moon, together with UK best selling author J K Rowling (31st July). Usually these people are the centre of attention and successful in all that they do. They are energetic and enthusiastic, tend to marry at a young age and their family is vitally important to them.

The late Roald Dahl, who thrilled so many people young and old with his stories, was influenced by the moon in Arbitration Time with his birthday being 13th September. This is a time when the harvest is waiting but plans need to be carefully put into place in order to make the most of it. Roald Dahl certainly planned ahead meticulously. He had his own little garden shed where he wrote and hated to be disturbed in his plotting and planning!

Those born under the Song Time lunation such as the late Johnny Carson (23rd October) and Hillary Clinton (26th October), work slowly and steadily to grow an abundant harvest, and are good communicators. Like these two examples, they often use their considerable skills in ovation to speak on behalf of those who cannot speak for themselves.

CELTIC TIMING – THE LUNATIONS

Moon	Season	Time
1st Moon	Seedfall	October/November
2nd Moon	Mid-Seedfall	November
3rd Moon	Darkest Depths	November/December
4th Moon	Cold Time	December/January
5th Moon	Stay-Home Time	January/February
6th Moon	Time of Ice	February/March
7th Moon	Time of Winds	March/April
8th Moon	Shoots-Show	April/May
9th Moon	Time of Brightness	May/June
10th Moon	Horse Time	June/July
11th Moon	Claim Time	July/August
12th Moon	Arbitration Time	August/September
13th Moon	Song Time	September/October

Figure 1, Celtic Timing – The Lunations

Chapter 2

An Introduction to Numerological Timing

Numerology, the science of numbers, has been with us for thousands of years, and was perhaps first developed by the Chaldeans, the prophets of Ancient Egypt, who lived at the time when the pyramids were being built. It is not a New Age craze. The symbolism of numbers has been an integral part of human living since our ancestors lived in caves, and these pre-historic people used numbers to communicate long before they developed what we now know as the alphabet. In fact it was the mathematician and philosopher, Pythagoras, who brought it to the fore in more recent times, and this is the basis for my interpretations as well.

I had not heard about numerology until I went to a hypno-therapist to get help to give up smoking. Even before I sat down, he asked me my date of birth. I gave it to him and he explained that the reason I smoked was because my Lifepath was Number 1, so that suggested I rarely felt that I fitted into groups, that I usually felt isolated from others, and therefore I took up the social act of smoking in order to be 'one of them',' one of the crowd'. This suggestion made perfect sense to me. I had always been the one who'd stand up and speak out, and rarely received any support from others, and although I was quite popular I never quite fitted in. From that moment I gave up my unhealthy habit of smoking, despite apparently being addicted to them for almost fifteen years! I was amazed that this stranger could so easily home in on an important aspect of my life, and naturally that experience gave me the impetus to explore the science of numbers more deeply for myself. As I delved into it my fear that I might need to acquire a PhD in arithmetic fortunately proved to be unfounded! In fact, to find the most important numbers in this science, all you need do is add two digits together at any one time. So 35 is 3+5 = 8, and 14 is 1+4 = 5. One of the handy things about numerology is that, once you become proficient at understanding and translating the symbols of the numbers, you can do it in your head, so there's no need for cards or pens or paper. It is through experience and experimentation that you will achieve success in understanding what each number means to someone. Below is a simple explanation to help you.

In this section I will be helping you to discover what your Lifepath Number is, which explains what you are meant to achieve while on Planet Earth, as well as the Personal Year that you are currently in. By learning about these numbers you can find out for yourself when it is best to change careers, why certain things didn't happen when you thought they should and, most importantly, the perfect timing for making certain decisions and when to take action and when to rest. I shall be looking at some well-known personalities to give you the opportunity to see how certain numbers relate to real people and it might help you to understand why they behave as they do at specific times.

It's all about 'perfect timing': doing what you are meant to do at the time you are meant to do it. Since discovering Numerology and putting it into practice in my own life, decisions have become much simpler for me. Now I know when to start something and when to do nothing, I know when to say "hello" to someone and when to say "goodbye". I tend to know when 'the check is in the post' and wait for it patiently without concern, and when I should demand payment.

Anyone who has had a reading with me knows that I strongly believe that we are here to learn lessons and move on after each lesson is faced and dealt with. To paraphrase the philosopher Anthony de Mello: "The joys of life can make us content and happy for a while, but it is only by facing the difficulties that we grow spiritually." The difficulties or lessons are shown in the date of your birth which is known as your Lifepath Number. Getting your number is quite simple, as mentioned above it is just a matter of adding two digits together. The numbers which have such significance in our lives are 1-9 and number 11. This number 11 is special, and when you come across it first you do not add up the two digits as with other numbers (i.e. 19 is 1+9 = 10, and 1+0 =1), but instead keep it as Number 11 until you add it to another number. (See below for examples).

Finding Your Lifepath Number

First of all we will find out your Lifepath Number, this will be followed by discovering your Personal Year, and we can finish with what I call the Universal Day number which affects us all on a daily basis.

The Lifepath Number

This is based on your date of birth. When you discover your Lifepath and follow it, this is the first step to finding happiness and fulfilment in all that you do. (The explanation for each number follows shortly).

As stated earlier, it's really simple to make these important additions as all you need do is add together two digits at a time. It is important, however, to add them up in the way shown below so that you do not make any mistakes.

Let's say you were born on 17th March, 1972. Write out the birthdate in this way: 17 03 19 72. Then add up the numbers in the way shown below, bringing all double-digits down to a single number, with the exception of the number 11. In the following example you will see how the numbers 1+9 = 10, and these two numbers are added together again, giving 1+0 = 1, and the figure 12 is 1+2 = 3.

1	7	0	3	1	9	7	2
	8		3	1		9	
		11			1		
			3				

Therefore, if you were born on the date shown, your Lifepath Number is 3.

So what is your Lifepath? To find out, simply add up your date of birth in the way shown above.

Now that you know your Lifepath Number, what does it mean? The following will give you some guidance of what your 'destiny' is, and what to try to avoid. We're all here to learn lessons so the quicker we learn them the better it will be for our progress. Are you doing what you should be doing? You'll know if you are, because you'll feel happy and successful. If you don't feel this way, what do you need to do differently to bring about a different result? Now let's see what you should be doing according to your Lifepath Number:

If you're a Number 1 Lifepath:

Even though you may feel that you never quite fit in, and long to be 'part of the crowd', remember that you are unique, so you are not meant to be a 'clone' of anyone else. You need to be independent and make your own decisions. In business you should use your initiative and take charge, for you are a natural manager and leader. You are probably inspired with brilliant ideas, and see possibilities where no-one else sees them. Generally, you have unusual ideas and tend to be about ten years ahead of others in your thinking. You will need to have a lot of faith in yourself and your ideas, for few people will see their potential.

It is important that you have your own space, but do not isolate yourself from others. In your early years you may feel lonely and therefore develop co-dependent relationships, feeling you cannot live without someone, or that you must do what everyone else is doing. When you feel lonely, remember these moments are given to you to help you learn to stand on your own two feet, being just yourself and no-one else!

If you're a Number 2 Lifepath:

Number 2 is about the ability to respond to events and also about how you relate to yourself and others.

It is about realising that no matter what is happening, you always have freedom to choose how you respond. Even if you decide to do nothing, that is a decision that you have made. For instance, neither you nor I can stop it raining, but both you and I can respond to it in a way that can be to our advantage: I can decide to stay indoors, or I can decide to travel by car or dress appropriately. You can do the same. So, although it rains, neither of us needs to get wet! We each have our own choice about how we respond to each and every situation. It is the very same in other areas, we cannot change anyone else, we can only change the response we make to that person or that event! It is important, therefore, not to fall into 'a blame game', where it is "everyone else's fault, poor me!"

The word 'relationship' is about how we relate to ourselves and others. If I do not respect myself I cannot expect other people to respect me. All relationships begin and end with how you relate to yourself.

Usually those with a 2 Lifepath are happier as part of a team – in marriage or business – for they yearn to share with others.

If you're a Number 3 Lifepath:

This is about three different things: emotional expression, creative expression and balance of body/mind/spirit. That means laughter and tears at the appropriate times. Bear in mind that hiding or suppressing your feelings can lead to depression. Should this happen, take a few moments to cry, shout or laugh and ensure your emotions are 'flowing' again!

15

Secondly, when you are a Number 3 Lifepath, it is vital to express yourself creatively. That can often be by giving birth to ideas and even giving birth to babies! Creative expression is mostly about having inspiration and imagination. Even drawing or doodling can be a form of creative expression. Remember, we create our lives, so be careful that you use positive words in order to create for yourself a positive life. Choose words such as 'joy', 'happiness', 'success'. 'health', 'wealth' and 'wisdom'. It takes exactly the same amount of time to be positive as it does to be negative, but the outcome is totally different!

As you mature, having a balance of body/mind and spirit will become more important to you. It will never be enough to have only physical fulfilment, or even mental agility. However, having a belief that you are here with a purpose and you can fulfil it will make you happy.

If you're a Number 4 Lifepath

The main 'lesson' for a 4 Lifepath is to become 'empowered. Having this Lifepath usually means you have a need to feel safe and secure, and you don't like sudden change. The way to self-empowerment is to become safe and secure through your own achievement and by facing your fears, rather than expecting someone else to support you. If you leave it up to someone else you almost certainly risk becoming a slave and feeling as though you are a prisoner. When you feel safe and secure you will be able to free yourself from fear and enjoy some adventures!

Becoming 'empowered' means working towards a long-term goal under your own steam, and facing any fear you might meet along the way. Remember, fear is just a thought, it is not a reality. It is okay to feel fear when facing something for the first time, but the secret is to face it! Often we might have a brilliant idea but our enthusiasm runs out before we can achieve our goal. It's important if you have a Number 4 Lifepath to work towards a long-held ambition, and to support yourself emotionally as you make the journey towards achieving it.

Often, people with a 4 can be bullied in their early years, or even be a bully! They are also hard workers, if not 'workaholics'. Perhaps you find it difficult to say 'no', and you may need to have to face some very bad behaviour before you get angry enough to say 'no', even if it means you risk being unpopular.

If you're a Number 5 Lifepath:

Number 5 is about the need for 'constructive freedom', in other words the need to let go of any self-destructive behaviour patterns. Often we pick up these from teachers, parents and siblings. While those patterns may have been perfectly correct for those people, they may not be the ones for you. We are all meant to live happy, fulfilled lives. When you are a 5, you need to look at any area where you are unhappy. How do you usually respond to the issue? If you're unhappy with the present outcome the only alternative is to make a change. Follow a different pattern and you will get a different result! See your life as though you're building a beautiful house. Start with the design and then the foundations....yes, it is hard work but it's worth it.

Number 5 is about facing the conflict of change, and seeing change as an adventure, not as something to be feared. Change is a natural process of life and, like the snake that sheds its skin in order to be reborn, we often need to shed our past and start afresh. The idea of change can often be frightening, while the act of change can often be exciting and adventurous. It's a matter of being open and flexible.

If you're a Number 6 Lifepath:

Number 6 is about the need for love and self-esteem. Perhaps you have tried to change yourself in order to please people? Perhaps you believe that you'll be loved only if you show certain 'acceptable' aspects of yourself? You will find that this doesn't work for very long, for the first way to get love is to accept it from yourself!

Self-esteem or self-love is not about being boastful or selfish. The only person who truly knows you is you, and if you can accept yourself, then you can accept others. Everyone feels they have 'faults', and accepting them is the first step to a healthy 'self-esteem'. No-one is perfect. We are not meant to be perfect. We're each here to learn certain

17

lessons, and it's okay to be 'imperfect' while we're on that learning curve!

Most likely you are a generous person and a good friend to others. However, it is vital that you do not allow yourself to be 'used' by anyone! You must respect yourself and tell yourself that you are doing 'the best you can'. Remember you can never do better than your best.

When you forgive yourself for not being perfect you will attract into your life wonderful loving, supportive people, who treat you well and share love and generous acts with you. However, if you do not forgive yourself, you may attract people who do not treat you well.

If you're a Number 7 Lifepath:

A Number 7 Person usually places a lot of emphasis on seeking and sharing knowledge found in education, academia, religion or science. Often you may feel that if you can't share what you know until you have a certificate or degree proving that you studied it. While it is always good to be open to learning things, you must not stop yourself moving ahead or sharing your knowledge simply because you are waiting to have the proof of it framed on a wall! As you move towards your 40s, the need for a 7 Lifepath is to open up to your 'intuition' which means 'tuition from within', i.e. learning from your spirit. When we want to know something from our intuition we are actually getting in touch with what we also call 'the Universal Mind' which knows everything.

Nurture 'an open mind'. Read books, query what you read and keep asking questions! The more you learn the more you can share with others. You would make a natural teacher, even if you're just having a chat with someone. You also need to learn to trust yourself, rather than trust someone else more than yourself. Otherwise, you may feel 'betrayed' by those you trusted, but you can only ever be betrayed by yourself, because you always had the answer inside, your intuition.

If you're a Number 8 Lifepath:

The figure 8 is two circles. The lower circle is about fulfilling your physical needs: (i.e. love, food, money, clothes, sex, house, car, affection, security and stability), while the upper circle is about fulfilling yourself spiritually (knowing you're here with a purpose, that you're doing something worthwhile). As you reach your 40s, more than likely your perspective of life changes. Buying clothes or having a nice car or a good holiday every year will no longer be enough. You will need more, for your spirit is checking if you are fulfilled. If you work only to make money, no amount of money will be enough. It's only when you are doing something that you feel makes a difference that you will find you always have enough. This is because your 'sense of worth' will attract 'worth' into your life. If you are doing something that is 'worth less', you will receive 'less worth'. We are each like magnets, we attract what we feel we are worth. Worth is about money, but also things that no amount of money can buy: health, wisdom, friendship, support, love, happiness, joy, etc.

Living an unbalanced life can cause all sorts of problems: 'retail therapy', over-eating, smoking, alcoholism, workaholism, etc. If you are constantly having health issues or financial problems, check out your lifestyle. The more balanced you are, the better your life will be.

If you're a Number 9 Lifepath:

When Number 9 is your lifepath number, you need to focus on communication, humanitarianism and letting go of the past.

You do not have to talk all the time, but you do need to talk about what is important. You may be very shy so your 'lesson' is to communicate your thoughts to others. It is also important to listen to what others are saying. Shy people are usually good observers, understanding what people mean behind the words they use. Though you may find it difficult to speak up for yourself, you may find it easier to speak up for others, whether for people, animals or the planet.

A humanitarian is someone who cares about the planet and all who live on her, working in ecology or with people who are disadvantaged. This can prove very satisfying, but it is also important that you remember to look after your own needs as well!

It is vital that you acknowledge what happened in the past, but let it go! Do not live in the past, for you cannot change it. Remember the saying: 'Yesterday is history, tomorrow is a mystery. The only moment that matters is now.' So acknowledge what happened in the past, but leave it behind.

If you're a Number 11 Lifepath:

Number 11 is about being 'a visionary', seeing what people can attain if they fulfil their potential. However, they probably are not able to see it for themselves or perhaps they don't have the courage to pursue it. This may cause problems in relationships, as you may believe someone is perfect, and then they show that they're not perfect and you are disappointed and frustrated! Learn to accept people as they are, remembering that everyone is human, and therefore imperfect. Think well of people, but let them be themselves. That also goes for you - don't judge yourself, remember you're human too!

You may feel 'ungrounded' at times because you find it easier to be in touch with spirit than in touch with Planet Earth ! Be open to spiritual development and spiritual guidance, through communications with angels and spirit guides. However, do remember that you are human and you are living a human experience so be practical, keep your feet on the ground. .

You may tend to be a perfectionist. Don't miss out on experiences just because you feel you won't achieve 100%. The joy of life is in the experience, rather than the outcome.

Those who are an 11 can also be futuristic in their thinking. Put these inspired ideas to good use, bring them into reality, and you can have great success.

Chart for Lifepath Numbers

No. 1:   Remember to be your own unique self. Make your own decisions. Be your own leader.

No. 2   It's not what happens, it's how we respond to what happens. Remember every relationship begins and ends with the way you relate to yourself.

No. 3   Express yourself both emotionally (through laughter or tears) and creatively (by dancing, singing, painting, etc). Balance body/mind/spirit.

No. 4   Face your fears, have a long-term goal and work hard towards it. Be stable and secure through your own efforts.

No. 5   Achieve 'constructive freedom' by facing what needs to be changed and taking positive action. Look on change as an adventure.

No. 6   Learn to accept and love yourself. Forgive yourself for being imperfect. Learn to say 'no' and don't allow anyone to treat you without respect.

No. 7   Be open to knowledge and different ideas, and pass it on to others. Learn to trust your intuition and have faith in yourself. Be patient.

No. 8   Have a balance between physical and spiritual fulfilment. Know that you are here with a purpose, that you need to do things that matter.

No. 9   Make sure you have your voice heard but also that you listen. Remember the need for humanitarianism, and for letting go of the past.

No.11   Allow your vision to see possibilities where no-one else sees them. Be realistic in your dreams. Seek perfection but accept imperfection.

Figure 2 – Chart for Lifepath Numbers

Some Celebrities and their Lifepath 'Numbers',

Let's take a look at some well-known media personalities to see what Lifepath they are to follow and what 'lessons' they will need to learn. You will notice that, while they may share their overall destiny or Lifepath with one another, the numbers (or 'lessons') which bring them to their destination are usually different. This is what makes each of our life journeys different from one another, though we often share certain elements with others for long or short periods.

A Number 1 Lifepath person often feels they do not fit into the norm and, when they allow themselves to do things differently, to stand out, they have great potential to reach Number 1, to achieve their highest goals. They need to be their own leader and make up their own minds, even if this can mean they are going against what everyone else is doing, for they are natural innovators and can even be seen as eccentric. Firstly, let's look at singer/songwriter Bruce Springsteen. His birthday is:

2	3	0	9	1	9	4	9
	5		9	1		4	
		5			5		
			1				

(Note. Keep adding up the double digits, i.e. 5 + 5 = 10, 1+0 – 1, except when the ultimate addition comes to 11, for we leave it at 11).

Someone else who shares this Lifepath number is the actor Stephen Moyer who plays the role of Bill Compton in 'True Blood'. His birthday is:

1	1	1	0	1	9	6	9
1	1	1		1		6	
		3			7		
			1				

If you follow the recommendations as shown above in order to work out the Lifepath Number, you will find that very few people who have a Number 2 Lifepath, which gives totally different lessons to those with a 2+9 = 11 Lifepath. (In fact, there will be no-one with this number born in the year 2,000 and onwards). People who have a Number 2 Lifepath tend to be quite co-dependent and see themselves through other people's eyes. Famous for being famous, socialite Paris Hilton is not someone who can live or thrive alone. She works best when she is involved within a team of some kind, whether it is part of a media campaign or working on a film set. Her birthday is:

1	7	0	2	1	9	8	1
	8		2	1		9	
		1			1		
			2				

Katy Perry and singer/songwriter Rod Stewart are both a Number 3 Lifepath. This is all about the need to express, whether by writing, acting, singing, dancing or painting, in fact any way that is creative and expressive. Of course, people with this Lifepath often need to learn to express positively, and may go through phases of being aggressive or depressive, rather than expressive. They may feel their emotions are blocked and often find an outlet on the stage. This number Lifepath often suggests a longing to become a parent.

Katy Perry's birthday is:

2	5	1	0	1	9	8	4
	7		1	1		3	
		8			4		
			3				

On the other hand, Rod Stewart's numbers are made up this way:

1	0	0	1	1	9	4	5
	1		1	1		9	
		2			1		
			3				

No 4 is all about focusing on a long term goal and working hard towards it. Canadian singer/actor Michael Bublé dreamed of being a singer since he was two years old. He explained in an interview with Oprah Winfrey that he had prayed on the Bible every night to fulfil his dream, and now he is an international star. Michael's birthday is:

0	9	0	9	1	9	7	5
	9		9	1		3	
		9			4		
			4				

Born into poverty in rural Mississippi, she is now the richest African-American in history and has been described as the most influential woman in the world. She could so easily have taken on the role of victim, but instead she focused on being a victor. She started in local media in her teens, but before long she had created her own niche as a chat show host and began to syndicate her own shows. The rest is history. Media star Oprah Winfrey is another Number 4 Lifepath who successfully worked towards a long-held goal. This how we make up her numbers:

2	9	0	1	1	9	5	4
1	1		1	1	9		
		3		1			
		4					

When you have a Number 5 Lifepath you will perhaps have a struggle finding your place in life and try many routes before finally constructing the role that suits you best. Number 5s are also multi-skilled and this, in itself, can cause problems because the question can be 'I can do so many things, but what can I do best?' 5 is also about 'facing conflict' rather than running away from what needs to be changed.

Angelina Jolie had some difficulties in her childhood as her parents divorced and she was estranged from her father for some years. In her teens she faced conflict as she wanted to be a model yet was jeered by her contemporaries as she was extremely thin, wore braces and glasses and, despite living in Beverley Hills, often had to wear second hand clothes. She is now seen as one of the most attractive women in the world, while she has also achieved several awards in her film roles, as well as becoming a writer and is also a Goodwill Ambassador for the UNHCR. This is how we make up her Lifepath:

0	4	0	6	1	9	7	5
	4		6	1		3	
		1			4		
		5					

Irish actor Colin Farrell is also a Number 5. Looking for freedom from 'rules', he dropped out of acting school in Dublin but quickly got a role in the TV series 'Ballykissangel' which launched his varied screen acting career. In his early years he was the 'bad boy' of Hollywood, and he spent some time in rehabilitation. However, facing the need to change he did so, and in recent years he has won a Golden Globe Award for his role in the film 'In Bruges' and, after his first son was diagnosed with Angelman Syndrome in 2007, he became an official games spokesperson for the Special Olympics World Games.

3	1	0	5	1	9	7	6
	4		5	1		4	
		9			5		
			5				

Number 6 Lifepath people usually long for approval from others and therefore often put themselves centre-stage. Singers Suzi Quatro and Britney Spears are both Number 6. Suzi Quatto, who is possibly more popular in the UK than is her homeland, the US, is also a songwriter and tv actress. She has been a recording artist since the 1970s and in more recent years took on a cameo role in television's 'Happy Days'. Britney Spears has been performing on stage since taking dance classes at age three followed by gymnastics and voice training. It wasn't long before she fulfilled her dream and became a teen pop idol in her teens. However, like anyone in the public eye who sees themselves only as good as their last interview, it is vital for those with a 6 Lifepath to work on accepting themselves as they are, apparent faults and all.

As you can see from their birthdates, though their overall Lifepath Number is the same, the individual numbers which make it up are different.

Suzi Quatro's Lifepath is made up as follows:

0	3	0	6	1	9	5	0
	3		6	1		5	
	9				6		
	6						

However, Britney Spears's birth date is:

0	2	1	2	1	9	8	1
	2		3	1		9	
		5			1		
			6				

Quite a few actors and actresses share similar numbers. For instance, the UK actress Keira Knightley and international star Julia Roberts are both the Number 7 Lifepath. This is about learning, which is essential if you are taking on the role of someone else who exists only in a film script, as well as the need to trust one's intuition. Choosing which film to do, which director to trust, are just some of the 'lessons' to learn for such people.

Keira Knightley's numbers are as follows:

2	6	0	3	1	9	8	5
	8		3	1		4	
	1	1			5		
			7				

While Julia Roberts was born on:

2	8	1	0	1	9	6	7
	1		1	1		4	
		2			5		
			7				

You will have noted that the secret to being successful when you are a Number 8 Lifepath is to have a balance both physically and spiritually. The easiest way to check this is to ask 'Am I doing something that's worthwhile?' Two people who live by this dictum are former President of South Africa, Nelson Mandela, and former President of Ireland, Mary Robinson.

Nelson Mandela was born on 18th July, 1918. Therefore his birthdate adds up as follows:

1	8	0	7	1	9	1	8
	9		7	1		9	
		7			1		
			8				

Though imprisoned for his opposition to apartheid in his country, instead of being forgotten, he became a symbol of resistance to racism while on Robben Island. On gaining his freedom after 27 years, he used his power to bring together the people of South Africa as one under the umbrella of 'The Rainbow Nation'.

Mary Robinson was a barrister and active in the Women's Movement in Ireland before she was voted in as President. Through her work she brought about many changes for people in her country, but she did not 'sit on her laurels'. Instead, she went on to become High Commissioner for Human Rights at the United Nations, and is currently, among other posts, involved in the World Justice Project. Her date of birth is:

2	1	0	5	1	9	4	4
	3		5	1		8	
		8			9		
			8				

Here is proof that 'doing things that matter' will always be a byword of Number. 8 people: On his 89th birthday, Nelson Mandela convened The Elders, a group of world leaders coming together to contribute their wisdom, independent leadership and integrity to tackle some of the world's toughest problems. Mary Robinson is one of the Elders.

What happens when people who share their Lifepath Number come together, does it make them more compatible? It can certainly draw people together because, on the surface at least, you would appear to have a mutual goal in common. Take Renee Zelwegger and Jim Carrey. They are both Number 9s, but look at how their numbers are made up. They have little they would agree on!

Renee's birthdate is:

2	5	0	4	1	9	6	9
	7		4	1		6	
	1	1			7		
			9				

Jim Carrey's birthdate is:

1	7	0	1	1	9	6	2
	8		1	1		8	
		9			9		
			9				

The Number 11 is the sign of a visionary, someone who can see what is not obvious to others. They tend to think of 'the higher good' rather than their own personal needs, and can be perfectionists. Because they tend to be 'other worldly' they can sometimes fail to be realistic and be hoodwinked by others.

Canadian poet, singer and songwriter Leonard Cohen is one of these special people. This is how his lifepath works out to a Number 11:

2	1	0	9	1	9	3	4
	3		9	1		7	
		3			8		
			1	1			

Another celebrity who is a Number 11 is US President Barack Obama. When virtually every country was reeling from the financial meltdown, the world looked out for a person with vision, who would make decisions for 'the greater good'. This is his birthday:

0	4	0	8	1	9	6	1
	4		8	1		7	
		3			8		
			1	1			

The Personal Year

As stated earlier in the verses taken from the Book of Ecclesiastes 3. 1-8 'To every thing there is a season, and a time to every purpose under the heaven… a time to plant, and a time to pluck up that which is planted …'

Most of our problems or mistakes are caused by bad timing. You might be doing the right thing, but are you doing it at the optimum time, or are you trying to force things to happen against their natural rhythm? Are you missing out on a wonderful chance of success by losing heart and not 'striking while the iron is hot'? When you know what you are meant to sow, and when you are meant to sow it, when you know what you are meant to tend or to reap, you will then be doing the right thing at the right time. In other words, you will be practising Perfect Timing.

The year you are in at present is known as your Personal Year. Your Personal Year begins on the day of your birthday each year. So, unless you were born on the 1st January, this is not the start of your new year.

Your Lifepath Number will always remain the same, and it will give you the 'destiny' in your life. However, when we reach our twenties (i.e. when we leave college or home and are able to make our own decisions), we begin to live in cycles of nine years.

Each of these nine years has a specific purpose. Think of it like this: you are given a new garden every nine years, and it's up to you to choose what seeds to sow, how you tend them and change them if and when is necessary, and then you reap the harvest within this cycle. During the ninth year, parts of the garden die down naturally. The empty spaces are then ready for you to sow them with new 'seeds' for the future, beginning the following year as the first of a totally new 9 year cycle.

The way to find your Personal Year is very simple. You just write out the full date of your last birthday, then add up the numbers. The final digit is your Personal Year within that particular 9-year cycle. Make sure you put down the date of the last birthday you celebrated, not the birthday you are expecting to have later in the year, or you will end up making a fundamental mistake.

31

Finding the Personal Year of Some Celebrities:

In order to discover the Personal Year, write out the date of the person's last birthday. Then add up the double-digits until you get the final figure which is the Personal Year Number.

Earlier, we saw that the actress Angelina Jolie has her birthday on 4th June. She would therefore be in a Number 4 Personal Year from her birthday in 2010 which is about working hard towards a long-term goal.

0	4	0	6	2	0	1	0
	4		6	2		1	
		1			3		
			4				

Her partner, Brad Pitt, had his last birthday on 18th December, 2010.

1	8	1	2	2	0	1	0
	9		3	2		1	
		3			3		
			6				

Currently being in a Number 4 year, Angelina may be seriously considering the long-term commitment of marriage. As Brad is currently in the year of love, (Number 6), it would be a good idea for them to actually tie the knot some time between 4th June to 17th December 2011. This is because during this time she is in her Number 5 Personal Year (which is about change) and he will still be in the Number 6 year.

My birthday is on 17th February. The last birthday I had was in 2010. Therefore, I write out my Personal Year as follows:

1	7	0	2	2	0	1	0
8			2	2		1	
	1			3			
	4						

So, at the time of writing this I am in a Number 4 Personal Year. What do I need to do this year? Well, it's about long term focus, working towards a goal and not being held back by any obstacles I might see in my path. So that's what I'm doing writing this book, putting a lot of effort into something which won't give me much return just yet, but if I invest my time now, the future harvest should prove very worthwhile!

TV star Stephen Moyer has his birthday on 11th October. Therefore, his last birthday at the time of writing this book was:

1	1	1	0	2	0	1	0
1	1		1	2		1	
	3			3			
	6						

He, too, is currently in his Number 6 Personal Year, which should be a very good time for his popularity. Of course, he may have moments when he wonders 'Where did I go wrong?' if the phone doesn't ring for a while. The 'lesson' is to accept himself as he is, rather than wait for others to 'approve' of him.

Sometimes we can unwittingly make the wrong calculations for the Personal Year by getting confused about the calendar year during which something happened. This can often be different to someone's Personal Year during which the event happened. For instance, Hillary Clinton announced she would run for president on 20th January, 2008. Her Personal Year at that time had begun on her birthday in 2007. Therefore we use this date to work out which year she was in at that time:

2	6	1	0	2	0	0	7
	8		1	2		7	
		9			9		
			9				

So, you can now see why her plans took off initially yet did not succeed in the overall scheme of things: her presidential campaign was launched in her number 9 year, which is the time to bring things to a conclusion rather than to initiate something new. However, after she entered the first year of a completely new 9-year cycle from 26th October, 2008, she began her new role as Secretary of State.

Your Personal Year and What You Should Do

Now it's time to work out your own Personal Year. When was your last birthday? Remember, if you have not yet had your birthday within this calendar year, then you must choose the previous year.

Write out your last birthday and and add up all double-digits together, including the number 11. Now check in the information that follows to discover your Personal Year, what you should be doing in it, and what each Personal Year within the 9-year cycle has to offer. Some items may be repeated from the Lifepath Numbers explanation, because 'the lessons' to be learned at this time can be similar.

The easiest way to understand the 9-year cycle is to imagine it as though you are given a garden to tend. During the first year it's a bit like moving into a new housing estate, there's just top soil and nothing has been sown. Therefore it is up to you, and you alone, to sow seeds, plant shrubs and trees, and mow the lawn. The more you look after it, the better it will be as the cycle comes to a natural conclusion over the following eight years. To make this garden truly a place of beauty and abundant growth you must work in the right seasons, have vision and also have plenty of faith in your plans. If you do all that you are guaranteed a wonderful harvest.

A Number 1 Year

This is the first year of a new 9-year cycle. You have a chance to start something new this year, or begin again on an old project if it didn't take off before. Seeing your life as a garden should help you have a vision for the future. You want the things you work at to bloom and bring you a great harvest. So it helps to be aware that whatever you do in this Number 1 Year is sowing the seeds for the following eight years in this cycle. Make sure you don't bring in any weeds from the last year!

Your Number 1 Year is all about your identity. Find out who you are this year. What are you meant to be doing in this life? If you start a new job or a new project this year you should find it easier to get into the swing of things. You'll find things just fall into place because this is the right time for new beginnings, so enjoy it!

A Number 2 Year

This is the second year of the current cycle. In a Number 2 year you are tending 'the garden' you have sown in your previous year. You want your garden to blossom and bring you a great harvest. A newly sown plant needs care, and a Number 2 Year is for co-operating with people and events, and being part of a team. It's also a year for making decisions. This year you can respond in a new way to get a new outcome!

A Number 2 Year is a good year for spending time with someone you love and building up a very strong relationship. In a family, make sure you show that you are part of their team, take time for other members and realise that it's quality, not quantity, that counts in the end.

A Number 3 Year:

In a 3 Year you must express your emotions and be creative. Be very aware of the words you use: if you say or think 'I'll never get that job' or 'I never have enough money' well, that's what will happen! Change your mind this year and imagine being happy and wealthy. Soon you'll find that that positive image becomes real in your life. It has certainly worked for me!

Be creative, be open about your feelings. Start a diary, paint a picture or paint the bathroom! Sing in the shower, dig the garden, dance in the dark. No-one has to know what you're doing. Cry when you need to cry, laugh when you need to laugh. Then you'll be creating a happy and healthy life. Of course one very important thing you can create this year is a baby!

A Number 4 Year:

A 4 Year is about hard work that helps you to become safe and secure in the long term. This year it's important to focus on what you want for the future, even though you may not achieve it just yet. It's the year when you dig the foundations for what you want to build in the years ahead. If you don't see the long term benefits, you might just end up working all the time, just like a slave. So set a goal and work towards it. This might mean you have to 'weed out' some things you started in your first year so that the more important things can grow.

In a Number 4 Year you need to 'feel the fear and do it anyway', and so break through any obstacles holding you back. Remember, a fear is just a thought, it doesn't have to become a reality.

A Number 5 Year:

In a Number 5 Year you've reached the half-way point in your 9-year cycle. If you've worked hard so far now you'll begin to see results, it's as though buds are beginning to show in your garden before they come into full bloom. A Number 5 Year gives you the chance to face conflict and so make some important changes. Often we hide from conflict and live in 'denial', pretending that everything is fine when, in fact, we're living in dysfunction.

A Number 5 Year is the year to get rid of a bad habit. Even more 'weeding' may be needed! If you smoke or drink too much, put up with bad behaviour, or repeat mistakes, you'll find it's easier to stop this year. So give it a go! Try to build a happy, healthy life from the foundations up, just as you would take care in building a great house or a beautiful garden.

A Number 6 Year:

A Number 6 Year is all about love and self esteem. It's vital to love yourself before you can accept true, unconditional love from anyone else. Self-esteem is how you see your own worth. Do you feel you're worthwhile? Do you deserve good things in life? Are your friends a reflection of this belief, or do they use and abuse you? In this year you may feel you deserve better than your present life and love. If so, don't accept second-best.

None of us is meant to be perfect. We can only do our best. Learn to laugh at yourself, and at life. Forgive yourself for past mistakes. Then you can love yourself, and truly love others.

A Number 7 Year:

A Number 7 Year is all about learning and being patient. There's so much to learn it seems like there's no end to it! You may like to study for exams this year, re-train in your career, or you may prefer to pick up a book on holistic living and spiritual development, and attend a course or workshop.

This is a good time to get other people's opinions, but make your choice based on your own instinct. Instinct is another word for 'intuition' which means 'tuition' that you get from 'inside yourself' from your spirit. When you follow your intuition you can be sure you're on the right road!

A Number 8 Year:

A Number 8 Year means it's harvest time! You've worked hard, you've planned things out, you've been patient and now you are going to reap your rewards. This is the year when you can bring in that abundant harvest you so deserve. All the work you've put into your present cycle will now pay you back. Open your arms to receive that abundance!

This is also a good year for buying or selling property, investing your money or cashing in your investments. Balance is important, so don't go over-board. It's also a year when you may find you need more out of life than just money, so do something that makes a difference. The Number 8 looks like two rings joined together, so it could be a good year for marriage!

A Number 9 Year:

This is the last year of your present cycle. Just like in nature, you'll find that in a Number 9 Year lots of things come to a natural end, though it may seem inexplicable when it happens. Look at a garden at the end of the year: everything seems to have died off and there's no new growth around. Yet the garden isn't dead, it's just resting. Your life is like the garden. You've done a good job and now it's time to take a break and a rest. Some people take a career break at this time. By doing this can you begin afresh in your next 9-year cycle.

This is the year to finish things. Make an extra effort to clear the desk, to clean the house, to finish off that project. Everything will work towards you finalising things this year, so try not to start anything that you want to last for a long time.

Chart – The Personal Years

No. 1 Year is about: Getting to know yourself and developing your own identity.. New beginnings. Doing something different.

No. 2 Year is about: Looking after what you began last year. Making decisions. Having healthy one-to-one relationships.

No. 3 Year is about: Being creative and expressing how you feel. Using positive thoughts and words in order to create a positive life.

No. 4 Year is about: Working hard towards a long-term goal. Facing your fears, breaking through obstacles and empowering yourself.

No. 5 Year is about: Making changes and facing conflict where change is needed. Recognising negative patterns and creating positive patterns.

No. 6 Year is about: Having a healthy self-esteem and confidence in yourself. Loving yourself and others. Romance.

No. 7 Year is about: Trusting your inner voice, your 'intuition'. Learning and being patient.

No. 8 Year is about: Enjoying your harvest. Doing things that matter. Being balanced between your spiritual and physical achievements.

No. 9 Year is about: Getting your voice heard and hearing others. Doing things that have been left 'on the long finger'. Clearing things from the past.

Figure 3 – The Personal Years

It can be a good idea, and prove quite constructive, to look back at some important events in your life and see what Personal Year you were in during that time. You might be surprised to learn that when you followed your instincts things went well, and this would be because you were taking the right action at the right time. In areas where you may have had to face disappointment, was it because you were simply in the wrong Personal Year for such actions?

Spend some time going back over some events which made an impression on you. Remember to work it out on the last birthday you had during the year the event happened. Therefore, if your birthday is 21 April and the event happened on 15 March, 2010, then to find the Personal Year at that time you add the date of your last birthday, i.e. 21+4+20+09, giving a total of 9, so the Personal Year would have been Number 9. However, if the event happened on May 4, 2010, with your birthday being earlier that year you would add 21+4+20 + 10 = 10 = 1, so it would have happened in a Number 1 Personal Year. If you have a few moments you might like to go back and check out some important dates in your life. It may give you a fresh perspective as to why things happened or didn't happen. You may even discover that, even without knowing it, fate helped you to practise 'perfect timing'

Your Seasons

As mentioned earlier in this book, you only need work hard for a short period every year, for when you work in tandem with the natural rhythm of your year you will find things naturally fall into place for you.

Your new year is the time to make new year resolutions. It's important to state to yourself precisely what you wish to have in your new year, so spend some time on the night before your birthday writing out a plan for the coming twelve months. It doesn't have to be in full detail, but by focusing on what you wish for it will help you achieve it more easily. Otherwise you may just drift into a new year and just as slowly drift out of it a year later, with nothing gained!

Just as in the pastoral year, your Personal Year is divided into four seasons: Spring, Summer, Autumn and Winter. You don't have to be an avid gardener to know that it's best to till the earth in the springtime if you want to enjoy a good harvest later in the year. By working within each season you can make sure you're doing the right thing at the right time! As your year begins on the day of your birthday, that is the first day of your Springtime. Each season lasts for three months.

Take my birthday, which is 17th February. The 17th of February is the first day of my Spring, and this lasts for three months until 16th May. The next is my summer, which runs from 17th May to 16th August. This is followed by my autumn which is from 17th August to 16th November, and the last season is winter, which for me is from 17th November to 16th February. Now work out your seasons and the following is what each means.

Spring:

Spring is the time for starting off new projects, for 'planting seeds'. Whatever I do in my Springtime I know I will be reaping the benefit of it later in my year. I must work hard in my springtime if I want to succeed, in fact this can be the most demanding season of the year, though I won't see many benefits for my hard work for some time. Therefore, I need to be patient and realise that it's not possible to enjoy my 'harvest' just yet!

Summer:

Spring is followed by Summer which, as mentioned above, in my case starts on 17th May and goes on until 16th August each year. When is yours? The Summer is the time when I am very busy and everything I 'sowed' is now beginning to grow. I might decide to 'weed out' a few things that aren't doing so well so that I can better tend the projects I want to 'blossom'. Summer is also a demanding time as everything is demanding my attention and I may feel overwhelmed. Still, I must work hard thinning, weeding and feeding, and still remain patient while I watch the blossoms begin to turn into fruit.

Autumn:

The next season is Autumn. My autumn begins on 17th August and lasts for the next three months, until 16th November. At last it's time to reap the rewards for all my hard work! The Autumn is the time to harvest all the things I worked on during my Spring and Summer months. If I've been patient then I'm going to benefit a lot. This is possibly my favourite time of my year! It's also a time when I need to think ahead to the winter and ensure I have stores enough to survive.

Winter:

If my Autumn has paid me back for all the hard work I put in during the year, then my Winter can be a time to sit back and relax and live off my winter store. My Winter is from 17th November to 16th February of the following year. During these three months I need to take time off to relax and plan ahead for next Spring. Some things will die down naturally, just like the leaves fall off the trees in Winter. It doesn't mean they're dead, it just means they're taking a break so that they can store up energy for the next burst of activity in the following Spring. That's what we all need to do, too, otherwise we can exhaust ourselves and therefore suffer illness. The secret is to plan ahead but don't plant just yet! Very little will grow in the Winter and you can be very disappointed if you waste a lot of energy. For many years I, like many others, tried to start new projects on January 1st, not knowing I was in my Winter season. It's no wonder they rarely succeeded!

When you work out your own seasons you begin on your birthday with your three months of Spring. Put the dates in your diary so that you'll know when to work and when to rest. If you look back over the previous years you may find, like me, that you may have been doing things at the wrong time. Now, armed with this new knowledge, you can start afresh!

The Universal Day Number (UDN)

Every day of the year has a number assigned to it. While it is of vital importance to you if this happens to be your birthday (because it becomes your Personal Year), the Universal Day Number (UDN) can also be used for making the right decisions on the right date.

It's just a matter of adding up the numbers of a particular day's date. Remember to write out the entire date including the year. Then, to save time and give you some instant information on a date proposed for a specific task, jot down the number in your diary for each day. This will save you time, worry and stress. Before long you will have got into the habit of checking what to do and what not to do on a specific date. Note: Each time the month changes the UDN skips either backwards or forwards to a different number, i.e.

3	1	1	0	2	0	1	0
	4		1	2		1	
		5		3			
			8				

Although there's only one day's change between 31st October and 1st November, see how the number for the Universal Day jumps backwards:

0	1	1	1	2	0	1	0
	1	1	1	2		1	
		3		3			
			6				

Note, when we change the year, there's yet another change to take into consideration:

3	1	1	2	2	0	1	0
	4		3	2		1	
		7			3		
			1				

0	1	0	1	2	0	1	1
	1		1	2		1	1
		2			4		
			6				

Chart for Universal Days – Recommended Action

UD 1: A good day to start something new.

A good day to have a 'first date'.

A good day to spend time on personal matters.

Avoid feeling abandoned or being selfish.

UD 2: A good day for spending time with a loved one.

A good day for co-operating with others.

A good day for decision-making.

Avoid a 'blame game' mentality, make a decision!

UD 3: A good day for having fun.

A good day for being creative.

A good day for expressing joy or sadness.

Avoid suppressing emotion and consequent depression.

UD 4: A good day for working hard.

A good day for focusing on future plans.

A good day to face a fear or limitation.

Avoid trying to control others or being too fearful to move.

UD 5:	A good day for making changes.
	A good day for discovering negative patterns.
	A good day for ensuring variety in your life.
	Avoid living in denial about what's happening in reality.
UD 6:	A good day for enjoying friendship and support.
	A good day for showing forgiveness and compassion.
	A good day for love.
	Avoid trying to please everyone, be true to yourself
UD 7:	A good day for learning from past experiences.
	A good day for trusting your intuition.
	A good day for learning something new.
	Avoid trusting everyone but yourself. Learn from mistakes.

UD 8:	A good day for accepting money.
	A good day for enjoying balance of spirit and physical.
	A good day for being energetic and healthy.
	Avoid over-spending and ensure you do something worthwhile.
UD 9:	A good day for communicating ideas and beliefs.
	A good day for humanitarian work.
	A good day for clearing away unnecessary things.
	Avoid staying silent or talking too much. Listen to others.
UD 11:	A good day for being inspired with vision for the future.
	A good day for communicating with spirit and angels.
	A good day for letting go of judgement.
	Avoid being unrealistic, keep your feet on the ground.

Figure 4 – Universal Days – Recommended Action

Chapter 3

Using Astrology for Perfect Timing

T he science of astrology is fascinating and very informative. If ever you've had a full Natal Chart Reading you'll know how much detail about the past, present and most likely future it can give you. To interpret the chart accurately, however, does take some study and understanding. However, even if you have very little knowledge or experience of astrology, there is one aspect that you can check for yourself and that is the influence of the Moon. There follows the charts for positions and phases of the Moon to help you understand the basic requirements for doing the right thing at the right time. (Full information on where all the planets are can be found in an Ephemeris, which is also available on the internet.)

More than likely you know your own zodiac Sun Sign, and you probably sneak a view of the forecasts in the newspapers and magazines. However, the Sun Sign (where the Sun was at the time of your birth) is only one aspect of who you are and what motivates you. In fact the Moon could be considered more important as it is the indicator of what we long for, what motivates us.

The Moon

It is a well-known and scientific fact that the phases of the Moon affect tides, the weather and a female's menstrual cycle (in fact, the word 'month' comes from 'menses' the plural of mensis, the Latin for 'month'). When we work in tandem with the Moon, its phases and the sign through which it is passing, we shall be working with the right energies at the right time.

It takes approximately two and a half days for the Moon to move through each sign of the zodiac. As it travels through each sign it takes on board the energy of that sign. It also depends on the phase of the Moon at that time. Every month there is a New Moon (otherwise known as a Waxing Moon). Which is followed in two weeks by a Full Moon and then that becomes the Old Moon (or the Waning Moon).

It's simple and logical to follow the best lunar energy by starting any new project at the New Moon. That's when your energy is young and light and energetic, and you should feel full of enthusiasm, ready for new beginnings. Work assiduously for two weeks as the lunar energies grow from the New Moon to the Full Moon. You will probably find everything falls naturally into place for you during this time, and you can manage to achieve things almost effortlessly. The Full Moon can also be a time when emotional matters come to a head: arguments can occur, industrial strikes can affect us, and fears can build up. However, it's not all about negative events! The Full Moon can also bring romantic matters to a head and you might get a pat on the back for the effort you are putting into your career.

Once you have passed the Full Moon you will probably find you are getting tired and dispirited. While people were being supportive earlier on, it may now seem everyone has disappeared from your ambit. That's a normal reaction as the energy is dying away as the Moon wanes in the skies above. There's little point in trying to force any issues just now. The energy levels are reaching their lowest ebb and it's a waste of time and effort trying to make things happen. Much better to take a break, have a re-think and make new plans for another burst of energetic enthusiasm once there is another New Moon! The Waning Moon is a time for sedentary work, for researching what you need, for clearing up the fine details of a project.

Chart for the Phases of the Moon

New Moon:	Time to put energy into new projects.
	Energy should be high.
	Enthusiasm should be at its peak.
Full Moon:	Matters come to a head.
	Wishes should be fulfilled.
	Arguments and passions arise.
Old Moon:	Energy is low.
	Making an effort can be a problem.
	Time to clear up loose ends.

Figure 5 – The Phases of the Moon

The Zodiac (Sun) Signs

This shows the dates when the Sun moves through each sign during its annual journey through the zodiac. As the Sun takes much longer to travel than the Moon, the dates are the same for every year. Should the Sun and the Moon be in your sign at the same time, you should have extra energy in the area to which it refers (see When the Moon is in Your Sign below).

Chart for the Zodiac (Sun) Signs

Aries: March 21 - April 20

Taurus: April 21 – May 20

Gemini: May 21 – June 20

Cancer: June 21 - July 22

Leo: July 23 - August 22

Virgo: August 23 - September 22

Libra: September 23 - October 22

Scorpio: October 23 - November 21

Sagittarius: November 22 - December 20

Capricorn: December 21 - January 19

Aquarius: January 19 - February 18

Pisces: February 19 - March 20

Figure 6 – The Zodiac (Sun) Signs

Remember the two weeks from a New Moon to the Full Moon is the recommended time to make an effort to get things moving. Don't expect much to happen if it's the time of the Waning Moon. The following is an explanation of the types of energies which will be supporting you while the Moon travels through each sign. So when you want to make the best of a situation, find out firstly what phase the Moon is in. If you want to start a relationship or a new project, is it conducive to such an activity?

Then check with the sign it is passing through: should you be focusing on improving your love life, taking a break, starting a new career or making home improvements? Or is it time to give extra attention to your friends and your family members?

When the Moon is in Your Sign

(Note: The period from a New Moon to the Full Moon is know as 'Waxing', while that from the Full Moon to the Old Moon is known as 'Waning').

When the Moon is in Aries

Aries is a Fire Sign and it is the first sign of the zodiac. Being the symbol of the pioneer, this energy encourages quick, decisive actions often in unusual areas that will bring an immediate result. It is best to focus on situations that involve the self and the personality, but be careful that you are not being selfish in your behaviour. Once you make the decision you must stick by it. It is a good time for facing personal challenges and beginning short-term projects which won't require much staying power as this fiery energy often bursts into action but can burn itself out very quickly.

Recommended activities during this Moon: spend time outdoors, enjoy intellectual discussions. Cut hair (if you want it to grow slowly) while the Moon is waning. Harvest crops when the Moon is waning. Have a health check. Start a passionate romance (when the Moon is waxing).

When the Moon is in Taurus

Taurus is an Earth Sign and it is the symbol of stability and long term planning. This is usually a time for putting your head down and working towards achieving something substantial and solid, where you can actually see the results of your actions. Taurus has a great affinity with money. Anything to do with financial activities, such as buying a property, requesting a salary increase, investing or speculating are usually recommended at this time. Other activities could involve focusing on a relationship or refurbishing your home with beautiful furnishings and décor. Just make sure you're not antagonising those around you by being too stubborn!

Recommended activities during this Moon: massage and other beauty treatments, start a new business, invest in good quality goods for the long-term. Buy a permanent home during the waxing Moon. Make a will in the waxing Moon. Get married while the Moon is waxing. Plant root crops such as carrots and potatoes. Start a romance that's slow to develop but rewarding (when the Moon is waxing). Buy stocks and shares.

When the Moon is in Gemini

Gemini, the sign of the twins, is about communication and money. Usually everything is very busy and pretty demanding when the Moon is going through Gemini. It's about learning, communicating, reading, writing, thinking…. In fact, being constantly on the go. Your head will be so full of information and ideas at this time it's likely you might overlook some important detail. Remember to check the fine print!

Recommended activities during this Moon: Advertise your services/ products, Cut hair (if you want it to grow slowly) while the Moon is waning. Harvest crops when the Moon is waning. Purchase a car, bake cakes, buy goods in a sale. Re-decorating and home repairs are recommended when the Moon is waxing, meet friends unexpectedly. Break a bad habit (when the Moon is waning). Have a party or attend one. Hire new staff during the waxing Moon. Enjoy air travel. Write creatively or write letters to friends and family.

When the Moon is in Cancer

The sign of Cancer shows a crab side-stepping an obstacle on its path. You may be tempted to live in denial while the Moon goes through this sign, but your problems won't disappear, they will re-surface. This sign is focused on domestic and maternal issues. You might find that family issues come to the fore at this time and you, and the people around you, may be more sensitive than usual. Arrange a social get-together and offer extra support to those in need.

Recommended activities during this Moon: Go fishing (after the Full Moon). Go fishing (after the Full Moon). (If you want it to grow quickly) during a Waxing Moon. Have a health check. Get married while the Moon is waxing. Plant lettuce, broccoli and cauliflower.

When the Moon is in Leo

Leo, the sign of the Lion, is one of the most fun-loving and childlike of the signs, and so when the Moon travels through Leo it's usually a time for having fun and being creative. You should find a supportive word and a smile works wonders, and new friendships can spring up at this time. It's a good time for having a party and/or spending time with children. It's often a time when you can be in receipt of some surprisingly supportive news in the workplace. Just restrain yourself from being a drama queen no matter how strong the temptation!

Recommended activities during this Moon: Entertain friends, break a bad habit (when the Moon is waning). Harvest crops when the Moon is waning. Spray pests and weeds during the waning Moon. Buy a permanent home during the waxing Moon. Make a will in the waxing Moon. Get married while the Moon is waxing. Have a party or attend one. Start a passionate romance (when the Moon is waxing).

When the Moon is in Virgo

The sign of Virgo is about being a perfectionist, of believing that nothing but the best will do, but it may be necessary for you to accept less than the best. It's about working hard, and being of service to others in a selfless manner. It's a good time to focus on following an intellectual pursuit for your mind should be clear and decisive. This is a time when commitment and integrity are integral to your needs, and you may find yourself being extra-critical of others, and even yourself, at this time. While it's important to follow best possible practise, try not to antagonise people by being overly fussy and demanding..

Recommended activities during this Moon: Visit the dentist. Cut hair (if you want it to grow slowly) while the Moon is waning. Start a romance that's slow to develop but rewarding (when the Moon is waxing). Bring home a new pet. Break a habit (at the waning Moon). Hire new staff during the waxing Moon. Start a diet during the waning Moon.

When the Moon is in Libra

Libra is about relationships, and often we may feel it easier to back off from facing disagreements while the Moon is going through this sign. Obviously, co-operation and compromise is often the best way to approach a problem, but if it keeps recurring it means you must face up to it, there's no excuse! How you get on with others in the workplace will also be high-lighted, and giving or accepting support is probably the answer at this time.

Recommended activities during this Moon: Re-decorating and home repairs when the Moon is waxing. Entertain friends. Have a health check. Become engaged during the Waxing Moon. Have a party or attend one. Start a romance (when the Moon is waxing).

When the Moon is in Scorpio

A Scorpio Moon is about several issues: sorting out your taxes or other accounting matters, it's also about sexual and intimacy issues, and research and self-awareness. It can be a good time to bring things to an end, as well as clearing out unnecessary possessions from your life. Sometimes, however, you might find it extremely difficult to let go, more so than when the Moon is going through other signs.

Recommended activities during this Moon: Go fishing (after the Full Moon). Make a will in the waxing Moon. Plant lettuce, broccoli or cauliflower. Fertilize your crops and flowers (when the Moon is waxing use chemical fertilizers, when waning use organic.)

When the Moon is in Sagittarius

A Sagittarian Moon is a time when you feel like taking off on an adventure, when you tend to take things to extremes. It's not good enough to feel fine, you have to feel either sublime or in the depths of depression! There is a tendency to use retail-therapy to get a 'hit' and go over the top either falling in love or else arguing with your lover.

Recommended activities during this Moon: Harvest crops when the Moon is waning. Have a party or attend one. Start a passionate romance (when the Moon is waxing). Enjoy air travel.

When the Moon is in Capricorn

Being an Earth Sign, this is about working hard towards a long term goal. Patience is required, but if you're willing to plan ahead and keep faith, the outcome should be most satisfactory. It's a particularly good time for someone who has ambition to make a move in their career and to look after things that keep you feeling safe, such as long term investments.

Recommended activities during this Moon: Have a health check. Purchase a car. Plant root crops such as carrots and potatoes. Start a romance that's slow to develop but rewarding (when the Moon is waxing). Advertise your business. Buy stocks and shares.

When the Moon is in Aquarius

Aquarian energy is about forward thinking and quite radical undertakings. This is an Air Sign which is about group projects, with an underlying belief of 'working towards the higher good'. It's a good time also for breaking the mould and doing something new.

Recommended activities during this Moon: Start a new building project, have a beauty treatment. Undergo re-decorating and home repairs when the Moon is waxing. Make new friends. Break a bad habit (when the Moon is waning). Harvest crops when the Moon is waning.

Spray pests and weeds during the waning Moon. Make a will in the waxing Moon.

When the Moon is in Pisces

Being a Water Sign this is a good time for looking after issues that lie beneath the surface, so taking on a journey of the imagination, such as being creative, can benefit you now. It's also a good time for following a spiritual path, for instance joining a workshop, meditating, reading books on the subject or even dreaming. People may feel rather sensitive just now, so don't step on their toes!

Recommended activities during this Moon: Working with others, taking advice from experts and consultants. Go fishing (after the Full Moon). Cut hair (if you want it to grow quickly) from New Moon to Full Moon. Plant lettuce, broccoli or cauliflower. Bring home a new pet.

The Phases of the Moon

The best way to discover the phases of the moon is to refer to an Ephemeris, a diary showing the moon phases, or check the charts below. However, you can gain quite an accurate reading of the lunar times by literally looking up at the sky at night. Then remember the saying: Light on the right means the moon is light, (i.e. it's new and waxing), light on the left, it's waning (i.e. the Old Moon). Sometimes you might find it quite confusing because of the different names the lunar phases are given: New Moon is also known as the Waxing Crescent, Increasing Moon, First Quarter, Gibbous Moon which then grows into a Full Moon. The next phase is about the Decreasing Moon also known as Last Quarter, the Old Moon, Balsamic, Waning Crescent and Dark of the Moon.

You'll know your Sun Sign but are you aware of the Sun Sign which is opposite yours? Check it out by counting six signs down from your own, so Aries is opposite Libra, Leo is opposite Aquarius. It may be that things tend to be more stressful when the Moon is in the opposite sign to your Sun Sign. Just be aware of this possibility and step back from troublesome issues at this time.

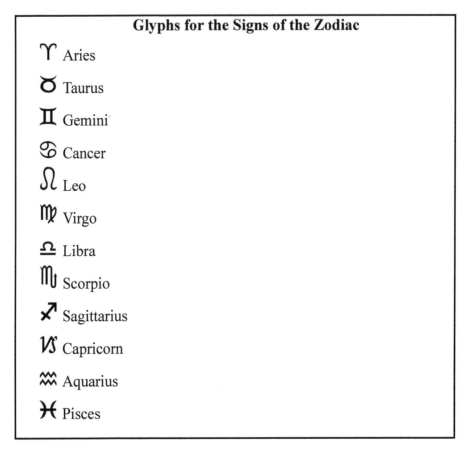

Figure 7 – Glyphs for the Signs of the Zodiac

2011 Phases of the Moon in the Northern Hemisphere			
NEW MOON	FIRST QUARTER	FULL MOON	LAST QUARTER
Jan 4 ♑	Jan 12 ♈	Jan 19 ♌	Jan 26 ♏
Feb 3 ♒	Feb 11 ♐	Feb 18 ♓	Feb 24 ♉
Mar 4 ♓	Mar 12 ♊	Mar 19 ♎	Mar 26 ♑
Apr 3 ♈	Apr 11 ♋	Apr 18 ♏	Apr 25 ♒
May 3 ♉	May 10 ♌	May 17 ♐	May 24 ♓
Jun 1 ♊	Jun 9 ♎	Jun 15 ♐	Jun 23 ♈
Jul 1 ♋	Jul 8 ♎	Jul 15 ♒	Jul 23 ♉
Jul 30 ♌	Aug 6 ♏	Aug 13 ♒	Aug 21 ♉
Aug 29 ♍	Sep 4 ♐	Sep 12 ♓	Sep 20 ♋
Sep 27 ♎	Oct 4 ♑	Oct 12 ♈	Oct 20 ♌
Oct 26 ♏	Nov 2 ♒	Nov 10 ♉	Nov 18 ♍
Nov 25 ♐	Dec 2 ♓	Dec 10 ♊	Dec 18 ♎
Dec 24 ♑			

Figure 8 – 2011 Phases of the Moon in the Northern Hemisphere

2012 Phases of the Moon in the Northern Hemisphere

NEW MOON	FIRST QUARTER	FULL MOON	LAST QUARTER
	Jan 1 ♈	Jan 9 ♋	Jan 16 ♏
Jan 23 ♒	Jan 31 ♐	Feb 7 ♌	Feb 14 ♏
Feb 21 ♓	Mar 1 ♊	Mar 8 ♍	Mar 15 ♑
Mar 22 ♈	Mar 30 ♋	Apr 6 ♎	Apr 13 ♒
Apr 21 ♉	Apr 29 ♌	May 6 ♏	May 12 ♒
May 20 ♊	May 28 ♍	Jun 4 ♐	Jun 11 ♓
Jun 19 ♋	Jun 27 ♎	Jul 3 ♑	Jul 11 ♉
Jul 19 ♌	Jul 26 ♏	Aug 2 ♒	Aug 9 ♉
Aug 17 ♌	Aug 24 ♐	Aug 31 ♓	Sep 8 ♊
Sep 16 ♎	Sep 22 ♑	Sep 30 ♈	Oct 8 ♋
Oct 15 ♎	Oct 22 ♒	Oct 29 ♉	Nov 7 ♌
Nov 13 ♏	Nov 20 ♓	Nov 28 ♊	Dec 6 ♍
Dec 13 ♑	Dec 20 ♈	Dec 28 ♋	

Figure 9 – 2012 Phases of the Moon in the Northern Hemisphere

2013 Phases of the Moon in the Northern Hemisphere			
NEW MOON	FIRST QUARTER	FULL MOON	LAST QUARTER
			Jan 5 ♎
Jan 11 ♑	Jan 18 ♈	Jan 27 ♌	Feb 3 ♏
Feb 10 ♓	Feb 17 ♊	Feb 25 ♍	Mar 4 ♐
Mar 11 ♓	Mar 19 ♋	Mar 27 ♎	Apr 3 ♑
Apr 10 ♈	Apr 18 ♌	Apr 25 ♏	May 2 ♒
May 10 ♊	May 18 ♍	May 25 ♐	May 31 ♓
Jun 8 ♊	Jun 16 ♍	Jun 23 ♑	Jun 30 ♈
Jul 8 ♋	July 16 ♏	Jul 22 ♒	July 29 ♉
Aug 6 ♌	Aug 14 ♏	Aug 21 ♓	Aug 28 ♊
Sep 5 ♍	Sep 12 ♐	Sep 19 ♈	Sep 27 ♋
Oct 5 ♎	Oct 11 ♑	Oct 18 ♈	Oct 26 ♌
Nov 3 ♏	Nov 10 ♒	Nov 17 ♉	Nov 25 ♍
Dec 3 ♐	Dec 9 ♓	Dec 17 ♋	Dec 25 ♎

Figure 10 – 2013 Phases of the Moon in the Northern Hemisphere

| 2014 Phases of the Moon in the Northern Hemisphere | | | |
NEW MOON	FIRST QUARTER	FULL MOON	LAST QUARTER
Jan 1 ♑	Jan 8 ♈	Jan 16 ♌	Jan 24 ♏
Jan 30 ♒	Feb 6 ♉	Feb 14 ♌	Feb 22 ♐
Mar 1 ♓	Mar 8 ♊	Mar 16 ♍	Mar 24 ♑
Mar 30 ♈	Apr 7 ♋	Apr 15 ♏	Apr 22 ♒
Apr 29 ♉	May 7 ♌	May 14 ♏	May 21 ♓
May 28 ♊	Jun 5 ♍	Jun 13 ♑	Jun 19 ♈
Jun 27 ♋	Jul 5 ♎	Jul 12 ♑	Jul 19 ♉
Jul 26 ♌	Aug 4 ♏	Aug 10 ♒	Aug 17 ♊
Aug 25 ♍	Sep 2 ♐	Sep 9 ♈	Sep 16 ♋
Sep 24 ♎	Oct 1 ♑	Oct 8 ♈	Oct 15 ♋
Oct 23 ♏	Oct 31 ♒	Nov 6 ♉	Nov 14 ♌
Nov 22 ♐	Nov 29 ♓	Dec 6 ♊	Dec 14 ♍
Dec 22 ♑	Dec 28 ♈		

Figure 11 – 2014 Phases of the Moon in the Northern Hemisphere

2015 Phases of the Moon in the Northern Hemisphere			
NEW MOON	*FIRST QUARTER*	*FULL MOON*	*LAST QUARTER*
			Jan 5 ♋
Jan 13 ♏	Jan 20 ♒	Jan 27 ♉	Feb. 3 ♌
Feb 12 ♐	Feb 18 ♒	Feb 25 ♊	Mar 5 ♍
Mar 13 ♐	Mar 20 ♈	Mar 27 ♋	Apr 4 ♎
Apr 12 ♒	Apr 18 ♉	Apr 25 ♌	May 4 ♏
May 11 ♒	May 18 ♊	May 25 ♍	June 2 ♐
June 9 ♓	June 16 ♋	June 24 ♎	July 2 ♑
July 8 ♈	July 16 ♌	July 24 ♏	July 31 ♒
Aug. 7 ♉	Aug. 14 ♌	Aug. 22 ♐	Aug. 29 ♓
Sept. 5 ♊	Sept. 13 ♍	Sept. 21 ♑	Sept. 28 ♈
Oct. 4 ♋	Oct. 13 ♏	Oct. 20 ♑	Oct. 27 ♉
Nov. 3 ♌	Nov. 11 ♏	Nov. 19 ♓	Nov. 25 ♊
Dec. 3 ♍	Dec. 11 ♐	Dec. 18 ♈	Dec. 25 ♋

Figure 12 – 2015 Phases of the Moon in the Northern Hemisphere

Mercury Retrograde – Some Sound Advice

Apart from the lunar influences as mentioned above, something important happens usually three or four times a year and this is when Mercury, the planet which rules the issues of communication, money and technology, turns 'retrograde' for a three week period. The purpose of Mercury retrograde is to review and revise your life and your connection with reality. Mercury travels very fast, and has an orbit that at times gets ahead of the Sun, thereby allowing you to see into the future and focus on new and innovative ideas. However, in order to bring these ideas into reality you must slow down and look after the nitty-gritty of what is required. It isn't enough to dream, you must do the basic ground work as well. When Mercury retrogrades back into the present, and is therefore no longer jumping ahead, you have the chance to test out your ideas and plans and see if they fit into your reality. This can often cause upset, delays and mis-understandings while everyone gets to grips with the new motion.

If you take a retrospective look at what was affected during earlier retrograde periods, you may discover there were new viruses let loose on the unsuspecting world, that your computer, telephone and other technological implements went on the blink for no apparent reason, that the 'cheque in the post' took a long time to arrive, workers go on strike and, generally, personal relationships took a beating due to unfathomable misunderstandings. It may sounds as though a lot of chaos erupts at this time, and this is quite correct. Fortunately, the problems usually only arise during the first couple of days when it intially turns retrograde and again when it turns direct three weeks later.

Take a look back at 2010. In 2010, Mercury turned direct on January 15th in Capricorn after approximately three weeks retrograde. This gave us the chance to review Capricorn-type issues, such as contracts and agreements. How did this affect you? There were four Mercury retrogrades in 2010, and each was in an Earth Sign. Firstly it was in Capricorn (turned direct on 15th January) which is about our business life. It turned retrograde from 19th April till 11th May in the sign of Taurus, which is about our financial support, and it went retrograde again on 21st August to 12th September in Virgo, which is about health. The last time it was retrograde in 2010 was yet again in an Earth sign, when it was in Capricorn, which is about work and family balance, from 11th to 30th December. Check back to see how Mercury affected you while it was in its retrograde cycle.

Mercury retrograde periods provide the opportunity to adjust your thoughts, attitudes and communications about your ultimate direction in life. The adjustments that occur in 2010 were in Earth signs, Capricorn (in January), Taurus (in May), Virgo (in Sept) and Capricorn again in December . These same signs at the same degrees were the Mercury retrogrades also experienced in 1931, as the cycle of Mercury retrograde repeats with an incredible exactness, activating the thoughts, ideas and communication processes which are needed by humanity at these given times. Of course looking back to that year it was just after the Wall Street Crash. Sound familiar?

In Greek mythology, Mercury is 'the messenger of the gods'. Astrologically, the planet Mercury is said to be associated with activities that relate to all forms of communications, travel, finances, and learning such as:

~ signing agreements
~ classes and schools
~ sending correspondence
~ technological implements, i.e. computers, radios, and phones
~ travelling and travel equipment
~ money

Therefore, it is recommended that the following activities are put on 'hold' while Mercury retrogrades:

~ making important decisions
~ travel, especially when there is a strict timetable
~ purchasing or using communications equipment (make sure you back up all files!)
~ signing contracts
~ agreeing business deals
~ sending important messages unless you double-check they have been received by the required party

~ starting any important project

However, it's not all bad news! As mentioned earlier, when Mercury is in retrograde it can be very helpful for the following activities:

~ Reviewing your plans and making any revisions to them.
~ Catching up on things you've left 'on the long finger'.
~ Getting rid of things you no longer need.
~ Re-considering issues that you may have been ignoring.

When Mercury goes retrograde it is strongly advised that you double-check all appointments, where to meet, the date and what time, the information you should bring with you, etc. It is quite amazing how appointments can get thoroughly mixed up and mis-understood at this time and these mis-conceptions can cause long-term problems in all kinds of relationships. Fore-warned is fore-armed!   If that isn't bad enough, the influence of Mercury retrograde can also cause travel delays (so double-check your passport, times of travel, boarding pass, etc), and general forgetfulness…. Fortunately the disruption doesn't usually last too long! While the retrograde action itself runs for three weeks, as mentioned the intermittent disruptions usually affect us only at the start and finish of the retrograde cycle. (See below for dates).

So, for the first day or so of its retrograde motion (and when it reverts to direct motion again) it is advisable to do as little as possible and try to defer any important meetings or agreements. Otherwise you are almost certainly going to hit some difficult times, with mis-directions, vagueness, mistakes and forgetfulness. Just recently in my own country, Ireland, when Mercury was retrograde a few months ago, a bank and a credit card company both found they had made small but significant errors on their customers' statements, and politicians have sometimes tripped themselves up with thoughtless words!   Keep alert to what happens in the media during the next retrograde and you may be stunned at how accurate this can prove to be!

It is also a good time to finalise some legal requirement. If this is the case, wait until the retrograde period to have another look at the situation. (However, avoid the start and ending of the retrograde motion, you will have at least the two middle weeks to take affirmative action). Slow down, take a good look and don't let anyone try to rush you. While it's a perfect time for revisiting old problems with a calmer head, it is not a good time to start a completely new project.

The following are the Mercury Retrograde dates for 2011-2015. I repeat, be very aware of the possibility of misunderstandings and delays occurring around the first and last dates of the retrograde period. (Note the planet moves at its own pace through the signs, and often reverts backwards into the previous sign when retrograde. It actually takes 88 days to orbit and Sun and passes through a zodiac sign every two weeks, so initially you may feel a little confused when you see the charts below. Remember Mercury travels at a different pace to the Sun.)

Mercury Retrograde dates for 2011

30 March	Mercury turns retrograde	In Aries
23 April	Mercury turns direct	In Taurus
2 August	Mercury turns retrograde	In Leo
26 August	Mercury turns direct	In Virgo
23 November	Mercury turns retrograde	In Sagittarius
13 December	Mercury turns direct	In Sagittarius

Mercury Retrograde dates for 2012

11 March	Mercury turns retrograde	In Aries
4 April	Mercury turns direct	In Pisces
14 July	Mercury turns retrograde	In Leo
7 August	Mercury turns direct	In Leo
6 November	Mercury turns retrograde	In Sagittarius
26 November	Mercury turns direct	In Scorpio

Mercury Retrograde dates for 2013

23 February	Mercury turns retrograde	In Pisces
17 March	Mercury turns direct	In Pisces
26 June	Mercury turns retrograde	In Cancer
20 July	Mercury turns direct	In Cancer
21 October	Mercury turns retrograde	In Scorpio
10 November	Mercury turns direct	In Scorpio

Mercury Retrograde dates for 2014

6 February	Mercury turns retrograde	In Pisces
28 February	Mercury turns direct	In Aquarius
7 June	Mercury turns retrograde	In Gemini
1 July	Mercury turns direct	In Cancer
4 October	Mercury turns retrograde	In Libra
25 October	Mercury turns direct	In Scorpio

Mercury Retrograde dates for 2015

21 January	Mercury turns retrograde	In Pisces
11 February	Mercury turns direct	In Aquarius
18 May	Mercury turns retrograde	In Taurus
11 June	Mercury turns direct	In Gemini
17 September	Mercury turns retrograde	In Virgo
9 October	Mercury turns direct	In Libra

Figure 13 – Mercury Retrograde Dates 2011-2015

It is also important to understand which area will be affected by the retrograde motion and this will be decided by the sign through which it falls. (You will see that Mercury does seem to often revert to the previous sign it went through when it goes retrograde. This is because the cosmos is still moving forward even though it seems Mercury is going backwards.) If you want to check out this with hindsight, look back at what was happening to you when Mercury turned retrograde in Taurus on 19th April 2010 and when it went direct again around 10th May. As it occurred in Taurus it would suggest it was affecting issues regarding home life, material comfort, money, food, and affection. On 21st August it turned retrograde in Virgo, and this could suggest issues regarding health and wellbeing. On 11th December Mercury turned retrograde in Capricorn. Family and security issues may demand attention and cause stress. As this latter date is the period covering Christmas, perhaps it gave time to renew the joys of family at this time. Being alert to these dates can help you sidestep difficult events and make the most of the helpful energies which are around you at this time. Below is a chart outlining possible problems arising when Mercury goes retrograde and is about to turn direct again.

Problem Areas When Mercury Retrograde

In Aries
Business deals, business start-ups, logic and reasoning, initiative and issues requiring will-power and staying-power.

In Taurus
Achieving concrete results for your work, buying and selling, personal security and financial dealings.

In Gemini
Intellectual ability and decision-making, communications through all media, travel arrangements.

In Cancer
Family relationships, parenting issues, imbalance in facing conflict.

In Leo
Tantrums and lack of reasoning debate, childishness, selfishness and feelings of abandonment.

In Virgo
Lack of efficiency, over-critical, lack of tolerance, overlooking small but necessary details.

In Libra
Unwilling or unable to co-operate with others, stubbornness, lack of diplomacy in communication.

Figure 14 – Problem Areas When Mercury Retrograde

In Scorpio
Unnecessarily secretive, self-destructive, overly-manipulative.

In Sagittarius
Judgemental and unable to see the other side of an argument, making impulsive and wasteful decisions.

In Capricorn
Self-discipline, family and work issues, problems relating to personal responsibility, inability to achieve goals.

In Aquarius
Unrealistic aspirations, misunderstandings in friendships, lack of organisation.

In Pisces
Feeling restricted and blocked, inability to focus, held back by past experiences.

Chapter 4

Using Lunar Magic

As explained in one of my earlier books, 'Angel Magic' (published by Element/HarperCollins), when you consider making your wishes come true through 'magic' it may make you feel a little fearful at first. This is because, throughout recent history, the idea of 'magic' has been transformed into something akin to fire and brimstone, darkness and hell. Often the very word 'magic' can conjure up fearful images of darkness, fire and brimstone, and anything else which portrays something sinister. This is because we tend not to understand what magic is and how it works. The best way to overcome any fear is to empower yourself with the truth behind the storytelling.

The word 'magic' comes from the Persian/Greek word 'magos', meaning 'sorcerer', someone who goes to the 'source' (or God) in order to empower things to happen. The word 'spell' comes from the French 'espeler' which translates 'to read out' or to 'name the letters of a word'. It has been known for many thousands of years that every word, especially when written, has enormous power. So, to make a magic spell simply means to go to God with your intention named out. In other words: 'Ask and thou shalt receive'.

You might wonder if magic is dangerous, does it not abuse or hurt people? No, it most decidedly does not hurt anyone, and it is not dangerous. Fiction writers and storytellers over the years have used their imagination to invent terrifying stories of fearful witches and warlocks, but they are all merely fiction. Fortunately we are now being encouraged to open our minds to knowledge and thereby take responsibility for own lives rather than live in ignorance and accept someone else's word as the truth. Using magic is simply about bringing your thoughts, words and deeds together with the gifts of God for the greater good.

Of course it is important that we do not abuse or manipulate anyone against their will, or cause them any harm. There is always the 'Universal Law of Ten-Fold Return' that must be considered, which means 'what you give out you will get back ten times stronger' so, if you wish distress on someone else, you are going to get that distress back ten fold into your own life, so it's definitely not recommended!

Have you ever wondered why we use candles in rituals whether in church or when making spells? When we light the candle we are asking the sun to come into our lives and bring us light, life and energy. Think about that the next time you light a candle, perhaps it will be to bring light, life and energy into a budding romance, or into a meditation. Unconsciously we are aware that there is something magical about candlelight, though we all have electric lights to live by, they simply aren't the same as candles when we want that to bring that 'added something' to a situation.

There is, of course, a recommended time to practise magic under the phases of the Moon. Firstly, the New Moon appears in your birth sign once a year. I'm an Aquarian so it's easy for me to be aware of it as it is the time of the Chinese New Year as well. You could buy a calendar showing the phases of the moon for future reference, or else refer to the charts earlier in this book. It's important to take a note of these special dates in your diary as certain times have more power than others. When the moon is in your sign around your birthday is a particularly potent time. This is when you can make new year resolutions, focusing on what you truly want and carrying out a ritual similar to that shown below.

There follows in the following chart a brief outline of the areas covered best by the moon phases:

Chart Showing Phases of the Moon

New Moon: Time for meditation, self-awareness and being inspired with creative ideas. Set goals and focus on them. Ask for the gift of clarity if you are unsure of what you desire.

First Quarter: Put your new plans into action. Set the foundations for the future success of the project and work hard towards your goal.

Full Moon: Ensure all the groundwork has been carried out and check on any small details you may have overlooked. Accept the support of your friends and colleagues, and spend some time socialising

Last Quarter: Slow down and take an overview of what you have achieved. This is a time for reflection rather than action. However, if you wish to free yourself from anything the energy of the Old Moon can help you let it go. It can also help you acknowledge what you need to leave behind.

Figure 15 – Phases of the Moon

If you want to cast a spell, i.e. focus on your wish, there are many books you can refer to, however, I believe that as it is all about the power of intention, there are some simple actions you can take to ensure your intent becomes reality. Making a spell requires your own wishes, a symbol of energy such as a candle (and using a specific colour and/or massaging it with oil as shown below can enhance your actions), and the wish literally spelt or written out on a piece of paper. This is what you need to do:

1. Decide on your wish.
2. Spend some time meditating to bring up your own power.
3. Provide a candle, preferably of the colour recommended below, or tie a ribbon of that colour in a circle around the candle, (but away from the candle flame due to risk of fire.)
4. Massage the specified oil into the candle: Be very aware of the power coursing through your body and into your hands as you do this. Keep your mind focused on your wish, visualise it happening if you can.

~ To ask for something/someone to come into your life massage the candle from the top to the middle and from the bottom to the middle;
~ To request that something/someone leave your life massage the candle from the middle to the end.

~ Light the candle, imagining sharing its power and light with you.
~ Write out on a sheet of clean paper your wish. Sign and date it.
~ Fold the paper in half, then quarters, then eights.
~ Burn the paper in the candle flame, sending it 'to the light'.
~ Let the candle burn out, or for safety reasons snuff it out and if there is any candle left bury it in the earth.

The Choice of Colour When Using Candle Magic

Blue: Communicating with people and other entities, for meditation and learning. Clearing blockages in communication. Enjoying peace of mind.

Brown   Issues involving the hearth and home, nature, and friendships.

Gold: Angelic help and help from heaven.

Yellow: Healing the body, bringing hope and happiness, freedom from negativity.

Green: Healing the heart, bringing financial prosperity. Achieving growth and personal goals.

Orange: Emotional stability, healing legal issues, healing relationships.

Pink: Love, romance, affection, forgiveness and healing relationships.

Purple: Spiritual healing, promoting psychic awareness and wisdom.

Red: For issues of passion, healing the heart and the need for courage. For career goals and issues requiring strong action.

Silver: Working with the energy of the moon (and female energy), for dreaming and developing clairvoyance.

White: For protection and clarity.

Figure 16 – The Choice of Colour When Using Candle Magic

As you handle the candle while meditating and making your spell, you are passing on your energy and intention and, by using one of the fragrant oils as specified below, you are adding the magical properties of that oil into your ritual. Here are some oils which might prove helpful:

Recommended Oils to use are as follows:	
Bergamot and	
Mint	Financial abundance.and good fortune.
Cinnamon:	Money, attraction between two people. Speeding up delays.
Frankincense:	Purification.
Geranium:	Fertility
Jasmine:	Spiritual love and to attract a man.
Lavender:	Peace of mind, healing and love.
Myrrh:	Protection and spirituality.
Patchouli:	Love, money, fertility and to attract a woman or a man.
Rose:	Attracting love, and good fortune.
Sage:	Wisdom and clarity.
Sandalwood:	Protection and spirituality.
Ylang Ylang:	Peace and spiritual balance.

Figure 17 – Recommended Oils for Lunar Magic

Some Simple New Moon Spells

For General Wishes

To carry out this spell you need to have 3 bay leaves, some paper and pen and a candle. (Choose the colour of the candle depending on the issue, see table above). It is best to carry this out at a New Moon. Any issue can be covered with this: love, money, career, home, etc.

1. Light the candle and gaze at its flame while you focus mentally on your wish.
2. Write the wish down on the paper. Visualise your wish becoming a reality.
3. Fold the paper into three, placing the three bay leaves inside. Again, imagine your wish coming true.
4. Again fold the paper a further three times, creating a secure square. Once more imagine your wish becoming a reality.
5. When you are ready, place the paper in a hidden place where it won't be disturbed for at least the full four weeks of the moon. Every day try to visualise your wish coming true. When it does, burn the paper and 'send it to the light' with thanks.

For Prosperity

Hecate is the Greek goddess of the moon, of magic, riches and wisdom.

This simple spell should be carried out at the time of the new moon. It is important that you are outside in the open when you perform this ritual, so that it feels as though you are in direct communication with the moon and its energy. You will also need to have some coins in your pocket or in your hand at this time, though the denominations are unimportant.

~ While you gaze up at the New Moon, turn the coins over in your hands and say the following either aloud or in your head three times:

'Hecate, goddess of magic, light and love, I pray
Bring good fortune to me this day.'

Then turn away and there is no need to ask again. Look out for new opportunities coming to you to enjoy some abundance!

Days of the Week for Making Spells

The following are what are known as Magical Days and are based on the Solar calendar. Try to carry out these activities on the days specified so that you can enjoy 'perfect timing' due to the increased energy given to the issue on that day.

Some Suggested Activities for Magical Days

Sunday: ambition, career, selling, speculating, children, crops, law.

Monday: issues involving water, dreams, travel, emotions, religion, reincarnation, spirituality.

Tuesday: business, partnerships, passion, physical pursuits, gardening, sexual activity, new beginnings.

Wednesday: advertising, communicating, book-keeping, editing, learning, travelling and writing.

Thursday long-distance travel, foreign investments and interests, philosophy, political interests, publishing, reading and learning.

Friday: artistic and creative pursuits, gardening, home improvements, event planning, dating and marriage.

Saturday: farming, hard work, clearing debts, shared money issues, housing, spending time with the elderly, tasks that require endurance.

Figure 18 – Activities for Magical Days

Gardening by the Moon

The recent financial downturn has had a positive effect on the health of at least some of our population who have decided to grow their own vegetables and fruit and therefore will benefit from eating the right foods which have been grown in the right natural rhythms of nature and are picked and eaten at the right time. Also, we have become more aware of all the free compost that is available to us if we gather our waste vegetable and plant matter and recycle it rather than send it to the local refuse dump. Of course, there is a specific time that is recommended for planting, nourishing, pruning, picking and recycling so that you can benefit from practising perfect timing.

Compost for a Good Start

The better your soil, the better your crop, and compost didn't get the name 'black gold' for no reason. It isn't just your waste materials but it also involves the hard work of worms, insects and other micro-organisms which bring about the organic magic that makes compost into the beneficial addition it makes to your garden. When making compost make sure you use a form of container that allows air in as well as moisture, and try to make it a mix of 2 parts brown material (dried leaves, dried grass clippings, dried coffee and tea dregs etc) to 1 part greens (mainly fresh, most waste such as new grass clippings, farmyard manure, fresh vegetable waste). It is important to turn the compost as this helps to improve the mix, gives more choice for the insects and worms, and therefore hastens the maturing of the compost heap.

The recommended times to start a compost heap are when the New Moon is in the Water Signs Cancer, Scorpio and Pisces. (Refer to Phases of the Moon as shown above for the current year.)

The recommended times to turn a compost heap are during the weeks of the Last Quarters of the Moon during any month, (see above charts for Last Quarters).

81

The following is a chart showing recommended times for sowing, planting and transplanting. Naturally there will be variations depending on your locality and the current weather conditions, so use your own experience and intuition as well when making decisions on these issues. It is also a good idea to keep a record of your own successes and failures so that you can learn from them in the years ahead.

~ Annuals (i.e. tomatoes, radishes, potatoes) are plants that need to be seeded each year as they complete their lifecycle within one growing season.

~ Biennials are those which are planted or seeded one year and need to grow through the winter and then produce their crop the following year (i.e. winter wheat and winter cabbage, etc).

~ Perennials grow from the same root each year, similar to bulb and root plants (daffodils, rhubarb, raspberry etc).

Chart for Lunar Gardening

From New Moon and

Second Quarter: Generally plant annuals that give their produce above ground such as broccoli, Brussels sprouts, cabbage, cauliflower, spinach, celery, lettuce, parsley, beans, aubergine, peppers, tomatoes. Roses, peonies, pansies, sunflowers, sweetpeas.

    This is also a good time for tending house plants.

From Full Moon

To 4th Quarter: Generally plant biennials, perennials, bulbs and root plants such as trees, shrubs, carrots, strawberries, beets, berries, cucumbers, radishes, turnips, leeks.

4th Quarter/

Old Moon   Onions, transplant tomato seedlings and others, destroy weeds and pests.

Figure 19 – Chart for Lunar Gardening

Some Weather Lore

~ While the above chart suggests the most appropriate time to sow and plant specific crops and flowers, the weather will also affect your ability to spend productive time in the garden, and in times of water shortages it would be helpful to plan ahead and therefore save water for essential gardening.

~ It is difficult to predict weather in the long term, but I have personally found the prediction of the Disting Moon to be very accurate in my locality. This is an old Norse weather marker, which occurs on 25th January each year and gives a reflection of what the weather will be like in your area around the time of the Summer Solstice (21st June) and Midsummer's Day (24th June). Every year on 25th January I take special note of what happens that day and I have so far found it to be quite amazingly accurate!

~ Literally standing outdoors at night time and looking up at the sky can give you a lot of information. Generally, you can predict short-term weather forecasts by watching what happens during the week of the New Moon. It tends to build up from the New Moon to the Full Moon and then the following two weeks will be similar but not as potent. So, for instance, if it is warm and dry in the first week it will most likely be warm and dry for the following three. Should you see a foggy mist obscuring a Moon (not clouds but a mist), you can be sure the weather is about to change, so beware and take affirmative action in your garden as required.

Chapter 5

Conclusion

So there you have it. You can refer to Celtic Astrology, Numerology, Astrology or all three to help you achieve 'perfect timing' for action-taking and decision-making in order to make your life more successful and less stressful.

If the only thing you take away from this is the knowledge of your own seasons and your personal year that would be a positive start. Remember you don't need to work the same way every day of the year; that is wasteful of energy as you would not be in synch with the natural rhythms of the Universe. Balance is necessary no matter what you are trying to achieve. That is, a balance or work and play, concentration and relaxation. Give your mind the chance to re-think your plans by sitting down and putting your feet up, or meditating on your problem before going to sleep.

While the information in this book is there to guide you and give you pause for thought, remember you have the ultimate self-knowledge deep inside you. By relaxing for a while and letting your intuition guide you it just may amaze you how far you can reach towards your ultimate goals!

For your own unique Lifepath Reading, using numerology, tarot and astrology,

contact me, Margaret Neylon

at Angelgate, Virginia, Co Cavan, Ireland

or email margaretneylon@eircom.net

http://www.margaretneylon.com

Lightning Source UK Ltd.
Milton Keynes UK
UKHW011327010920
369165UK00001B/100